Transformed
by
Love

*(The Story of
the Song of Solomon)*

Kevin King

ISBN 978-1-62137-099-4   First Edition, 18/2/2012.

ACKNOWLEDGEMENTS

It has been my wish to make this book available as widely as possible with a minimum of restrictions on its reproduction, by whatever means. But it was also my desire to include the text of the song itself, so that the reader would see this before reading my own comments.

Unfortunately, the quoting of entire books of the Bible presents copyright problems for the publishers of most modern translations. To avoid these, I found it necessary to choose between using an older, less readable, translation, or producing a rendering of the Song in my own words. I opted for the latter, as it let me take account of the combined wisdom of many translators and scholars rather than being tied to a single version. It is difficult to know how to properly acknowledge the efforts of so many translators when I have at the same time been consciously endeavouring not to plagiarise their work. All I can reasonably say is that my sources have included, but not been limited to, the American Standard Version, Authorised Version, Darby, Green's Literal Translation, LXX – An English Translation, New International Version, New King James Version, Revised Standard Version, Russian Synodal Translation, Young's Literal Translation, Young's Analytical Concordance and the Hebrew lexicons of the New American Standard Version and Online Bible.

Only when this book was almost complete did I come across the World English Bible (WEB), which is being produced specifically for the purpose of making a modern translation freely available in the Public Domain. Had I known of this at the outset, it is unlikely that I would have bothered with my own version: but having done so I decided to stick with it. However, I am delighted to have discovered the World English Bible and applaud the efforts of its translators. I have therefore made use of the WEB for all quotations other than those of the Song itself, unless otherwise stated.

CONTENTS

PREFACE

There are times in our lives when we go earnestly seeking after God; and there are times when God simply takes hold of us. Although this book is written as an encouragement to us to seek after Him, I can only begin by confessing that it is not the result of my spirituality in seeking God: but of his love, in taking hold of me.

In January of 2003 the church of which I was a member was going through hard times: but, as had been customary for many years, we began the year with a 'week' of prayer and fasting – well, a few days, at any rate. Oh, I was firmly convinced of the value of prayer and fasting, and resolved to participate as fully as practicable: but the most I was really hoping for was some clearer insight into the way forward for ourselves and the church.

Then God stepped in. I could not attempt to describe this intervention, without in some way cheapening it: suffice to say it hit me with the force of a spiritual earthquake. Apart from my conversion, 38 years previously, it was the most life-changing experience I have ever had: and left me in a state of spiritual shell-shock for months afterwards.

I began seeking God more earnestly than I had done in years. It was like being back in spiritual primary school: and one of the first lessons the Lord began impressing on me was the need to rediscover my first love. In one sense, that was not difficult: I was now spending two to three times as long in prayer as I had done previously; and finding even then that it never seemed enough.

But where should I turn to learn how this relationship was meant to be? I felt the Lord leading me to look again at the Song of Solomon. Day after day, I would be amazed at the things He showed me through its pages. I read it, meditated on it, and re-read it.

At first, that was all I could do. I had no idea what to do or expect next. I had been due to go on a teaching trip to a Bible School in South America: but now there was only one subject on my heart, and I was manifestly unfit to teach it. The trip was cancelled.

But gradually I began to get a sense that, somehow, God wanted me to act as a catalyst; encouraging others to also seek a deeper intimacy with, and commitment to, Himself. After a month or so, I began sharing some of the lessons I had been learning from the Song with the folk in our church. I would like to say that there was an instant revival – but there wasn't; though folk were blessed and challenged by the message. So I went on seeking God, frequently returning to the Song for fresh insight and encouragement.

A year later, I finally made that trip to South America; still very much as a novice learner in the school of faith and love, but making the message of the Song the prime focus of my ministry. A good number of the students testified that it had challenged and encouraged them. One, all unknowing, brought a prophecy that told me to use the pen that God had put in my hand. This, and other encouragements, finally persuaded me that this sense that had been growing in my spirit was not just my own idea.

The first draft was completed in 2004, Since then I have expounded this theme many times, made some revisions and added an epilogue. But the substance remains the same. So I now offer this book, confident of its message and praying that the Holy Spirit will take it and use it to encourage you, as He reveals to you the depth and intensity of his love *for you*, and its transforming power in your life.

Kevin King, February 2012.

INTRODUCTION

About Solomon (1:1)

¹The Song of Songs, by Solomon.

The opening verse attributes this song to King Solomon, who was a prolific song writer and noted for his great wisdom. This alone would make it very special: but the expression, 'Song of Songs,' signifies that there was something about this song that made it more important than any other. It can't have been the melody – it isn't even recorded – so what is it about this song that makes it so exceptional? It is my hope that you will find the answer to this for yourself as the story unfolds.

> Even if Solomon only meant it was the best of his own songs, this would be quite some claim; for 1 Kings 4:32 tells us that he wrote 1,005 of them!

One who knew the grace of God

Solomon was the heir of King David, who had been anointed by God in place of Saul, Israel's first king. But Solomon's choice as king, above that of David's older sons, is an amazing example of the grace of God. He was David's second son by Bathsheba; who had been the wife of Uriah the Hittite, one of David's military commanders. David had committed adultery with her and then, on learning she was pregnant, arranged for Uriah to be put in a battle situation where he was sure to die; subsequently marrying Bathsheba. One of the consequences of this appalling act was the death of the child; and one could easily have supposed that God would not want the offspring of such a union to have any place in his future plans for Israel.

But the grace of God is so powerful that it utterly disregards our past, and sees only the potential we have to become in Him. When Solomon was born, God again sent to David the very same prophet that had pronounced the death sentence against their first child. But this time it was to give Solomon a very special name, 'Jedidiah' – 'beloved of God.' (For the full story, see 2 Sam 11:1–12:25.) So Solomon grew up with a deep awareness of the life-changing, destiny-shaping power of God's grace.

His wisdom

David appointed Solomon his heir when he was near death, with his older sons competing for the throne. But when God offered to give Solomon anything he wanted, his request was for wisdom to rule God's people well. In response, God not only made him the wisest man that ever lived, but also gave him wealth, honour and long life (1 Kings 1:1-53 & 3:5-28).

His downfall

But, no matter how great and sincere they may be, wisdom and good intentions cannot preserve us if we rely on them to keep us from evil, rather than simply depend on God and obey his Word.

As we will discover, Solomon's Song reveals an amazing vision of kingship and love. But it is a vision that goes far beyond the ability of any mere man to fulfil; and part of Solomon's error was to think that he could do so.

Long before, God had warned Moses that any future king must not *'multiply wives to himself, that his heart not turn away'* (Deut 17:17). Disregarding this, Solomon married one wife after another. When he wrote the Song, he already had 60 wives and 80 concubines (Song 6:8): but he ended up with 700 wives and 300 concubines!

Solomon was a skilled diplomat: and he made many alliances by marrying daughters of foreign kings. Such marriages were even more expressly forbidden because of the idolatrous practices of the surrounding nations. So, by accepting the gods his wives worshipped, and even building shrines for them, he further undermined his own relationship with God.

> **What's a concubine?**
>
> A concubine was a wife of secondary rank, typically a slave.
>
> Though not having all the legal rights of a true wife, she could still attain great status in the household, if she found favour with her husband.

The result is that the book of Ecclesiastes shows him, as an old man, bemoaning the folly and emptiness of so much of his life. Also, as a direct result of his excesses, the kingdom was split in two during the reign of his son, Rehoboam (see 1 Kings 11:1-13).

Why is it in the Bible?

Many have asked this question. After all, it's a love song about a man and woman that scarcely even mentions God. And the descriptions used in places are very sensual – in fact, the Jewish Rabbis considered it unsuitable for anyone under the age of 30! Nevertheless, they recognised that the book contained a portrayal of love as it was meant to be; and wisely saw that a true understanding of love had to be an integral part of our relationships with one another and with God.

And what of the conduct of its author? Many of us would have been inclined to exclude Solomon's writings on this ground alone. But one of the lessons we learn from the Old Testament is that *all men are flawed: yet despite this God uses us to accomplish his purposes*; and even the least worthy may at times display deep spiritual wisdom and insight.

The style of the Old Testament is frequently to simply record what people did or said, with little or even no moral comment. The careless will simply read it, and pass on: but the wise will ponder the implications and consequences of their actions and learn. As Paul says, *'Every Scripture is God-breathed and profitable for teaching, for reproof, for correction, and for instruction in righteousness, that the man of God may be complete, thoroughly equipped for every good work.'* (2 Tim 3:16-17.)

More than a love song?

Many Rabbis viewed this song as an allegory of the relationship between God and Israel: and Christians, for their part, have seen it as an allegory of Jesus and the church. For Solomon, as I have already hinted, I think it was a vision of kingship and love. But, though it exceeded the capacity of any mere man to fulfil, it *is* perfectly and completely fulfilled in one person, and one person only – Jesus, the King of Love.

Who is it about?

Various suggestions have been made for the identity of Solomon's bride, ranging from a simple shepherdess, through Abishag the Shunamite, to Pharaoh's daughter or the Queen of Sheba. I very much doubt this was Abishag: but I also doubt that she was of royal birth, for reasons we will discuss later.

> Abishag was a sort of half-wife to David in his old age and is known to have been exceptionally beautiful (1 Kings 1:3-4). But the link to this song is tenuous, being based entirely on a similarity between 'Shunamite' and 'Shulamite' in 6:13.
>
> It is very unlikely because it was considered the ultimate insult for a son to take his father's wife (see 2 Samuel 16:21). Abishag's marital status may have been in doubt: but when Solomon's older brother Adonijah asked to marry her, Solomon had him summarily executed for merely suggesting it (see 1 Kings 2:13-25, *cf.* Lev. 20:11, Gen 35:22 & 49:3-4). And if Solomon had planned to marry her himself, it would probably have been early in his reign: not when he already had 60 queens and 80 concubines (Song 6:8).

A shepherdess then? Well, yes and no…

Who is speaking, and to whom?

The book has three main characters:
- The king, Solomon.

- The woman, referred to as the Shulamite in 6:13. I will refer to her as 'the Seeker,' because that is what she is doing – seeking to be closer to her king.
- The Daughters of Jerusalem, who could be described as the 'King Solomon Fan Club' – a band of young women who follow the king wherever they can. They want him to notice them: but their love is more superficial than the Seeker's.

One of the many difficulties in interpreting this book is the fact that it is not always clear who is speaking at any given moment. Where there is particular doubt, I will try to explain the implications of the differing viewpoints.

Problems of translation

There are two particular areas of difficulty when translating this book.

Firstly, the subject-matter means that some of the words, expressions and allusions are used only rarely, or not at all, in other surviving Hebrew literature. In such cases, scholars have to attempt to deduce their meanings from other words that appear to come from a common original or 'root' word.

Secondly, the book is written in verse. This means that the choice of words and phrasing is partly determined by the rhythm of the verse itself. Consequently, some of the words chosen are not those that would normally be used, or else are used in unusual ways. It is not possible to translate the song into English verse without further confusing its meaning: but users of some translations will see that the original lines are kept separate or, as in the New King James Version, the start of a new line in the original is marked with a capital letter.

Scholars do not always agree on the best translation. In making the version that accompanies this text I have concentrated on the narrative, not attempting to render this as verse, and generally followed the scholarly consensus as to the meaning. Where there are particularly significant disagreements between scholars, or where I am inclined to follow a minority opinion, I have tried to explain the alternatives and why I prefer one above another.

But that is enough introduction for now. Let's look at the song itself…

HUNGRY FOR LOVE (1:2-6)

It's the Way You Love Me (1:2-3)

The things you do (1:2)

²*May he kiss me with the kisses of his mouth!*
  For your lovings are better than wine.

Right from the outset, our seeker makes it clear to anyone who will listen that she is hungry for intimacy with her king. She doesn't just want to be one of those who admires him from a distance.

But the reason she gives the king is particularly revealing: though the English translation does not do it justice.

I occasionally travel to Russia, and have an elementary knowledge of Russian. So, in an effort to make up for my lack of conversational partners, I frequently read from the Russian Orthodox Bible. I was doing this when I began this study; and this verse brought me up short, sending me scurrying for my Russian dictionary – because the word it used here for 'love' was one that I had never seen before. I discovered that it meant 'caresses.'

In fact, the Hebrew uses the plural form of a word, *'dowd,'* that we will discuss in more detail later: but which roughly translates here as 'lovings.' When used in this way it includes the concepts of both physical acts of sexual love (such as caresses) and practical actions motivated by love. But the key point to grasp is that she is not talking about the *fact* that he loves her, but about the *way* he loves her.

It is wonderful to know that someone loves you: but the truth is that much of the time such knowledge stays in our heads and doesn't really stir our heart and emotions. However, when people *do* things that demonstrate how much they love us, theory comes alive. We *feel* loved, and are motivated to love them in return.

I have been very happily married now for over thirty years to a very wonderful wife. But one of the important lessons I have learned is that, if I really want to stir up her affections for me, the most successful strategy is not to make big speeches or dramatic gestures, and certainly not to simply assume that she should know by now that I love her. Instead, throughout the time that we are together, I will look for little things that I can do to show I care; a quick kiss or hug here, a helping hand with the chores there, and so on… Maybe at first she won't notice what I'm up to: but sooner or later she will – and the cumulative effect is well worth it!

It is just the same in our relationship with Jesus. As we become more intimate with Him we experience his love, not just as a fact to be believed, but as a daily awareness of the countless ways in which He lavishes his love on us: and the more aware we become of this, the more our own love is stirred. But if we fail to develop this intimacy then, although we may still acknowledge his love as a matter of spiritual truth, it will feel more like a theory than a fact to us.

The blessing you bring (1:3)

³*Because of the fragrance of your excellent oils, your name is like out-poured oil. The virgins love you.*

Wherever the king went, the fragrant oils with which he had been anointed would sweeten the air. And his liberality meant that those in his court would also receive whatever they needed, regardless of expense. This was so typical of him that the very mention of his name would evoke powerful memories of the sweetness of his presence, and stir a maiden's heart with desire for him.

But notice also the honesty of this particular admission. No doubt, as king, he was entitled to the devotion of his subjects: but the truth of the matter is that he is desired because his presence brings blessing.

In the same way, it is undoubtedly true that we should revere God's name simply because of who He is. But the reality is that, *'We love him, because he first loved us.'* (1 Jn 4:19.) I never really loved God, or was capable of loving Him, until I began to understand just how much He had done for me.

Drawn into his chambers (1:4)

4Draw me! We will run after you!
> *The king has brought me into his inner chambers.*
> *We rejoice and are glad in you. We will remember your lovings*
> *more than wine. They are so right to love you.*

Renderings of this verse vary, depending upon the translator's interpretation of who is speaking, and when. Some translations suggest this verse is spoken partly by the seeker and partly by the Daughters of Jerusalem. For my part, I incline to the view that the Seeker is speaking both on her own and the daughter's behalf.

I would suggest that there are three vital principles at work here.

The King must do the drawing

Firstly, all translations acknowledge that she needs the king to take the initiative. If he did not, she would have no hope of coming anywhere near him (the king's guards would have seen to that!) and any thoughts of true love would be nothing more than a pipe-dream.

Indeed, if he had taken no interest in her, she would probably never have loved him at all. Forced to only view him from a distance, he would have seemed so privileged and remote, that in time her feelings would more likely have tended towards envy than love. But all that changed the day he smiled on her. If the king wanted her, who dare stand in her way?

But she isn't just speaking of a single action. Her words imply an ongoing sense of her need for him to go on drawing her; and a commitment on her part that, if he will only do this, she will keep on after him.

In the same way, we also need God to take the initiative by his grace and stir our hearts if we are to truly seek Him. Jesus said, '*No one can come to me unless the Father who sent me draws him.*' (Jn 6:44.) The idea of a mere man having an intimate personal relationship with the Being who created this universe – compared to whom we are less than a speck of dust – would be unthinkable, were it not that He has taken the initiative in calling us to Himself.

Also, the weakness of our human nature is such that, without constant encouragement from Him, our love will all too easily fade and grow cold. But, just as she pleads with her king to draw her, so we can ask Jesus: and find He has already promised to respond: '*Ask, and it will be given you. Seek, and you will find. Knock, and it will be opened for you.*' (Mt 7:7.) '*Come to me, all you who labor and are heavily burdened, and I will give you rest.*' (Mt 11:28.) '*The Spirit and the bride say, "Come!" He who hears, let him say, "Come!" He who is thirsty, let him come. He who desires, let him take the water of life freely.*' (Rev 22:17.)

If I am drawn, others will follow

The traditional rendering of the opening words is, 'Draw me – we will run after you.'[1] This implies that, if the seeker is drawn by the king, others will be inspired to follow him too.

Put simply, passionate love is infectious. This principle can actually be seen in action later in the song.

---

[1] The literal rendering of these words is, 'Draw me – after you – we run.'

I am doubtful about the alternative rendering of 'we run' as, 'Let us make haste.' It would seem a bit premature for her to be telling the king to get a move on at this stage in their relationship. But nor is there any obvious reason to suggest that these words are interjected by the king.

Reader, please hear this. This book is about you and your relationship with God. You need to get your eyes off everyone else and onto Jesus.

If you are in Christian leadership, this can be really difficult (it can be even if you are not!) But, as a Bible teacher, no sooner did God start showing me something new from the song than I found myself mentally composing a sermon, telling people all about it! And God has had to repeatedly bring me up short on this, telling me to forget about teaching others and learn these lessons for myself.

(That is why the trip to South America had to be cancelled, and why it was over a year since God began showing me these things before I began to feel I could start working on this book. Not that this means I have finished learning. I know now, more deeply than ever, that you can never finish learning about the love of Jesus; and the only effective way of introducing others to his love is to be ever more filled with it myself.)

I'm acutely conscious that one of the chief maladies of Western Christianity is that we have lost our first love for Jesus, and I long to see it restored. But, although it may be possible to exhort and cajole people into submission to God, it is impossible to cajole them into loving Him. Many have burned themselves out trying.

But if we will stop trying to figure out how we can persuade others to love God more, and instead let Him stir our own hearts to follow Him more passionately, our love will become contagious. We will reproduce what we *are*, not what we *say*.

The King wants me as a personal friend

The word translated as 'inner chambers' doesn't mean the ceremonial halls, where the king would hold his royal courts and banquets: but neither is it his bedchamber. It means the private inner rooms where the king would spend time with his close friends, trusted servants, advisers and his own family. By bringing the seeker here, Solomon was declaring that she had become his trusted, personal friend and confidante.

Think of it! This was a favour far greater than being invited to sit at the king's table and drink the king's wines at a banquet, heady as such an experience might have been (in more ways than one!). Many a famous and noble guest at the king's banquets would never pass the portals into his inner rooms: yet here she was, being drawn into such a relationship.

One of the most amazing things that the Bible teaches is that the Almighty God wants the same kind of relationship with us. It is not enough for Him that we are his subjects: He wants us to be his family, friends and confidantes.

If you come from a Christian background, it should not surprise you to hear that God wants to be your friend; for the Bible is full of this message, from God's original communion with Adam (Gen 2:19) through Abraham, the friend of God (Gen 18:16-33), Jesus, who taught us to call God our Father (Lk 11:2), and on to the closing chapters of Revelation (Rev 21:7). But those from a non-Christian background may well be staggered by such a claim.

To some, God is far too exalted, and man far too insignificant by comparison, for God ever to acknowledge him in such terms (see, for example Bilquis Sheik's wonderful testimony, 'I Dared to Call Him Father'). And a Buddhist's concept of God is too impersonal. For many modern scientists also, the universe seems far too vast and impersonal for man to have any significance at all.

And yet, logically, a God of such awesome power must be capable of having a personal relationship with us, if He wants to; just as a king may make a friend of the very lowliest of his subjects, should he care enough to do so.

This is the greatest privilege of them all. But even so it is all too easy to overlook this and be seduced by lesser things.

It may seem superfluous to say that such an expression of love was of far more value than even the very best of the king's wines. Yet, there were probably many in Solomon's kingdom who would have valued a place at his banqueting tables – the thrill of the occasion, the adulation of the onlookers, and the sheer pleasure of the food and wine – more highly than a place in those inner rooms, where no-one else can see you. It is so easy to end up loving the gifts more than the giver.

There is a tragic irony here. For Solomon clearly saw the temptation that his riches presented to those on whom he lavished them. He wanted them to love him, and to be his true friends; not just to love the things he provided for them. And so in his song we have the seeker and Daughters of Jerusalem saying, 'We will remember your lovings [it is this word, *'dowd,'* again; meaning, *'acts of love'*] more than wine.' In saying this, he presents the best possible antidote to such seduction. It is that they should regard every blessing, whether of wine or friendship, as an act of his love, inspiring them to deeper love for the lover.

Yet it was this that Solomon himself ultimately failed to do. It is clear that in his youth he enjoyed an intimate relationship with God. But he became so preoccupied with affairs of state, and his affections for his many wives and subjects, that in the end they meant more to him than the love of God, who gave him them. So he ignored God's wishes in pursuing his own; and his relationship with God grew cold.

But Solomon is only one example of many who have confused God's blessings with the reality of personal intimacy. Samson thought that all was well as long as the Spirit's anointing gave him strength. Saul was more concerned about keeping the good opinion of the people than that of God. Peter, on the mount of transfiguration, fell so in love with the glory of that place that he did not want to leave; and had to be reminded of his primary duty to hear and obey God's Son.

And it is still true today. We can experience great personal blessing and emotional highs during times of public praise and worship, and in Divine visitations, when God makes his royal presence felt amongst his people. Some may receive great adulation because of the mighty ways they have been used as servants of God. But we need to realise that it is our intimate experience of God – expressed in the obedience that flows from this, and our desire to be available for Him in the 'inner rooms' of our prayer life, where only He sees us – that is the true measure of our love and really shapes our destiny.

I'm not worthy… Yes, you are! (1:5-6)

⁵I am black …
  – But lovely, O daughters of Jerusalem!
  Like the tents of Kedar …
  – Like the curtains of Solomon!
⁶Do not gaze at me, because I am black, because the sun has seen me.
  My mother's children burned against me. They made me keeper of
  the vineyards: but my own vineyard I have not kept.

These next two verses are crucial to our understanding of
who the Seeker is, and of the events that unfold in the song. But,
as there is some debate about who speaks when in verse 5, we
will look first at verse 6.

Despised by her Family (1:6)

It is immediately clear that she is not at all happy with
either the colour of her skin or her social status. She tells us her
brothers (quite possibly her sisters too, as the word used can
include both) had turned against her (literally, 'burned' against
her), forcing her to work in the vineyards.

This was hot, outdoor
work; and her skin would have
suffered badly from the sun,
wind and flies. Her weather
beaten complexion would have
contrasted sharply with those
of the elegant, leisured ladies,
who would normally be
expected to grace a king's
palace; and it was clearly a
source of deep embarrassment
to her.

We are not explicitly told
why her siblings were against
her: but the context raises the
possibility that this also may have been to do with her colour.

> The treatment of younger children described here was probably not unusual in large households.
>
> For example, when Samuel went to Jesse, Solomon's grandfather, to find the new king of Israel, David was out working in the fields. He also was apparently held in such low esteem that Jesse did not think of him, even when all his other sons had been rejected, until Samuel asked, *'Are all your children here?'* (1 Sam 16:11).

It may be that she was darker-skinned than they were; perhaps a half-sister, or even illegitimate. We have already noted that intermarriage of Israelites with foreigners was strongly discouraged, on account of their heathen practices: so if she had been foreign or half-caste, even if legally so, this would have been a further serious disadvantage to her.

> Some suggest the Seeker was the dark-skinned Queen of Sheba. But the picture we see here is not that of a queen; and certainly not that of the fabulously wealthy, highly-spirited woman who came to test Solomon with hard questions (1 Kings 10:1-2).

A number of commentators treat her words, '*my own vineyard I have not kept,*' as an admission of personal failure and neglect. But we need not think so harshly of her. Given what we see of her position as a despised minor daughter, it is very unlikely she would have had much to call her own; much less a vineyard. Thus her words are a plain statement of fact, expressing her sense of deprivation. In effect, she was little more than an unpaid servant, working in a vineyard destined to be inherited by others.

What comes across very clearly from this verse, is that she has a very low opinion of herself. Though she longs to be with the king, she is struggling with a deep-rooted sense of her own unworthiness. But there is hope for her: because rather than hide her problem, she is honest enough to admit it.

Loved by her King (1:5)

Given this information, let us look again at verse 5. We now know that, when she calls herself 'black' or 'dark,' she does so with a sense of shame. When she says she is '*like the Tents of Kedar*' she is referring to the tents used by the nomadic Arabian tribes, which were made from dark goatskins. Being constantly exposed to the desert dust, their outward appearance was very drab and unappealing: so here, again, she is running herself down.

But interspersed with these, we find two wonderfully affirmative statements, '*but lovely, O daughters of Jerusalem*' and,

'Like the curtains of Solomon.' Is she trying to counter her own self-criticism? If so, why would she immediately undo her first effort with another negative statement, and then ruin her second with an apology for the colour of her skin?

I believe these are not her words: but the king interrupting her, objecting to the negative things she says about herself. When she complains of her colour he declares to all the daughters of Jerusalem that, as far as he is concerned, she's beautiful. Then, when she compares herself to the scruffy tents of Kedar, he again contradicts; comparing her instead to his own magnificent curtains. He is probably also subtly pointing out that you should not judge by outward appearances; because, despite its drab exterior, the tent of a wealthy chieftain could be fabulously luxurious on the inside!

Many of us have a deep sense of inadequacy, worthlessness and rejection. Some of these feelings come from wounds inflicted by others; some are inadequacies we seem to have been born with; and some are self-inflicted. But often, we are so fearful of what others would think of us, if they only knew, that we put on a false front; pretending our problems don't exist – afraid even to face up to them ourselves.

But it was when she acknowledged her problem that the king sprang to her defence. If she had not admitted how she felt about herself, their relationship would have continued as a kind of charade. She would have been pretending there was nothing wrong with her complexion, yet all the time feeling, 'He must have noticed. What does he really think about me?' And he, for his part, would undoubtedly have noticed both her complexion and the tell-tale signs of her embarrassment. He would have been longing to tell her that it really didn't matter: but the subject would have been taboo, by her own choice. All he could do would be to go on telling her he loved her, knowing he was only half-believed, until such time as she was ready to face the issue.

In the same way, for as long as we deny our needs, we deny our King the opportunity to speak into our lives and deal with them.

It didn't really matter what anyone else thought if the king declared her beautiful! Even her past pain and disgrace didn't matter if her future lay in his hands.

Many years ago a good friend of mine, Kevin O'Neil, made a very profound comment about the difference between the love of God and the love of man. It is a long time since we last met, but this has stuck with me ever since...

> **The difference between the love of God and the love of man is that man loves people or things *because* they are precious: but God simply loves us – and by loving us *makes* us precious.**

Why is this? It is because, essentially, the value of any person or thing is defined by the price someone is prepared to pay for it.

The Incas and others often used to make cups and plates from a soft metal that was fairly abundant in some parts of their realm. It was too soft to be of much practical value for anything else, and it was rather heavy; so its only other use was for making ornaments. When the Europeans came, the Incas happily traded it for beads and other trinkets. But they were being conned. Today no-one, from Fort Knox to the Amazon jungle, trades beads for gold; for all know the true price that men are prepared to pay for it.

And your value is defined by the price someone was prepared to pay for you. To Jesus, we were precious enough to die for! This is a simply stunning, mind-numbing thought: that the Creator of the Universe (for that is who He is) should consider us so precious that He would do such a thing for us. But *what* a value it puts upon our lives!!

When Jesus says you are precious to Him, you *are* – no matter what anyone else may say.

THINGS ARE ABOUT TO CHANGE (1:7-11)

I want to be like You (1:7)

7Tell me, you whom my soul loves, where do you graze (your flock); where do you make it rest at noon. For why am I like one that is veiled beside your companion's flocks?

The stories about King Solomon tend to emphasise his wealth, leaving the impression that he spent all his time holding court in his fabulous palaces: but this is a rather one-sided view.

Despite all his riches, Solomon cared passionately about the state of the land, his people and his flocks. Throughout the period up to and including this song, at least, he involved himself directly in attending to their needs, investing a great deal of time and energy outside the palace walls.

We see evidence of this in his plea to God for wisdom to rule his people. And we can also see many indications of his love of the outdoor life both in his proverbs and in this song.

> *'Know well the state of your flocks, and pay attention to your herds: for riches are not forever, nor does even the crown endure to all generations. The hay is removed, and the new growth appears, the grasses of the hills are gathered in. The lambs are for your clothing, and the goats are the price of a field. There will be plenty of goats' milk for your food, for your family's food, and for the nourishment of your servant girls.'*
>
> (Prov 27:23-27. By Solomon, according to Prov 25:1.)

For example, 1 Kings 4:32-33 states that he told 3,000 proverbs, speaking *'of trees, from the cedar that is in Lebanon even to the hyssop that springs out of the wall; he spoke also of animals, and of birds, and of creeping things, and of fish.'* Now in those days there were no nature encyclopaedias or wildlife documentaries. Yet men did not go to Solomon's teachers to learn of these things: they came to him (1 Kings 4:34). It was he who had gathered all this knowledge: and the only way he could have done it was by spending a vast amount of time out in the wilds himself, observing first-hand the ways of the natural world and sharing the company of others who did the same.

Also, throughout the song itself, we see references to Solomon as a man who was constantly out and about, at all hours of the day and night; attending to his flocks, visiting the farthest corners of his realm, delighting in the wild places of the land, seeking gifts for his bride and caring for his people.

In short, Solomon was a Shepherd King.

Our seeker longs to be like him, near him, doing what he does. Her life as a vine dresser held little appeal for her: but it holds even less now.

It seems that she also has charge of some goats (see v.8). These are more self-sufficient than sheep, so it takes less skill to care for them. But this is her chance: if only she can find out where the King will be pasturing his flock, she could take her goats there too. Noon would be a good time: nobody goes anywhere much in the noonday heat. It would give her chance to get near him, stay near him, learn from him, become a shepherdess…

But it doesn't work out that easily. It seems that the king's companions won't say where they are going; so instead she goes to the king and asks him to tell her, saying, 'why am I like one that is veiled beside your companion's flocks?'

Note that she does not say she was actually wearing a veil: rather that she might as well have been.

The implication is that she has been discouraged from associating with them. As in many Islamic societies today, it appears that veils were particularly common at that time amongst married women. It was considered·highly improper for a man to spend time talking to someone else's wife; so they probably just ignored her, hoping that she would go away (as in the AV rendering, '*why should I be as one that turneth aside … ?*').

Jesus portrayed himself as the ultimate Shepherd King. He calls us his sheep, and we are his constant concern and delight. What is more, He actively encourages us to share in his work of caring for his flock.

> *I am the good shepherd. The good shepherd lays down his life for the sheep.*
>
> *… I know my own, and I'm known by my own; even as the Father knows me, and I know the Father. I lay down my life for the sheep. I have other sheep, which are not of this fold. I must bring them also, and they will hear my voice. They will become one flock with one shepherd.* (John 10:11,14-16)
>
> *Feed my sheep.* (John 21:17)

But, sometimes, those of us who are already following Jesus are too quick to find fault or suspect the motives of those who, to our mind, aren't seeking or serving Jesus the right way.

Maybe we don't like the way they dress, or their language. Maybe we think their behaviour is inappropriate, or their motives or opinions unsound. All too easily, like Solomon's companions, we can end up discouraging these seekers and causing them to turn aside. That is a tragic mistake, and one we must learn to guard against.

> *John answered, "Master, we saw someone casting out demons in your name, and we forbade him, because he doesn't follow with us."*
>
> *Jesus said to him, "Don't forbid him, for he who is not against us is for us".* (Luke 9:49-50)

First, learn to be a Sheep (1:8a)

8If you do not know, O fairest of women, go out after the tracks of the flock, …

The King, on the other hand, is delighted by her desire; and he encourages her by telling her yet again how beautiful he thinks she is.

Even so, he won't tell her where to go either. Instead, he tells her to follow the flock; because there is a vital principle at stake here:

> *If you want to be a good shepherd, then first you must learn to be a sheep!*
>
> **There can be no short-cuts.**

One of the key differences between Eastern shepherds and their Western counterparts was that the Eastern shepherd did not *drive* his sheep: he *led* them. For such a relationship to work, there had to be a deep bond of trust between shepherd and sheep. He had to understand their needs and reactions intimately, and they had to look upon him as one of themselves – the most trusted member of their flock.

So, the first lesson of shepherding she had to learn was how to be a sheep. She had to understand what it feels like to be a follower:

- to surrender your own will to the needs of others;
- to take your direction from others when you don't know where they're going;
- to trust that things really will be for the best when you distinctly remember something better back there;
- and so on…

Jesus is delighted by our desires to serve Him. But that doesn't mean that He will endorse all our plans.

We often dream of serving God and doing great things for Him. But we can never be truly effective for Him until we have learned to humble ourselves, and follow Him in simple trust and obedience; not as a leader, but as a follower; not as a ruler, but a servant. Because the essence of Christian leadership is completely unlike that of the ordinary secular or religious world – it is a leadership based on servanthood.

Consider Jesus again for a moment. Here was the Messiah; come from God and chosen by God to rule his people and proclaim the Gospel of God to them. Yet He was not permitted to begin this ministry until He was about thirty years old, and then it lasted a mere two to three years. Virgin-born and sinless, who could have been been better equipped for this task than He was? Yet He was required to spend thirty years in submission to his parents (see Lk 2:51) – *ten times* as long as He spent in leadership!

> Jesus summoned them, and said, "You know that the rulers of the nations lord it over them, and their great ones exercise authority over them. It shall not be so among you, but whoever desires to become great among you shall be your servant. Whoever desires to be first among you shall be your bondservant, even as the Son of Man came not to be served, but to serve, and to give his life as a ransom for many."
>
> (Mt 20:25-28)

If even He needed to do this, how much more do we?

Then, labour in the shade of his tents (1:8b)

8... and graze your kids beside the shepherds' tents.

N.B. the standard Hebrew word for 'shepherd' literally means, 'one who grazes.' It's actually the same word as in 'graze your kids' – not so much a title as a job description.

Shepherding is about function: not position. It doesn't matter what you are called or what recognition you get. A true shepherd is too busy caring for others to worry about that.

Tending the flock in the heat of the midday sun would be an exhausting experience: but he makes it easy for her. He tells her to stand beside the shepherd's tents. Here, she can still feed her kids, but at the same time find welcome shade and protection from danger.

Note that these are the *King's* tents. Far too often, our labour for God is so much harder than it ought to be, because we have allowed ourselves to wander away from his tents. If only we would focus more on keeping close to Him, we would find our service so much less of a trial to us. This is a picture of service based on a place of *rest*: not of striving in our own strength. Reaching that place in God may take an effort (it probably will): but from that position we can minister effectively without exhaustion (see Heb 4:1-11).

Nor is it just a place of rest; it is also a place of *safety*. Who would dare molest her here, beside the king's tent? What wild animal would dare come here? And if any did, what would happen to them?

I have found this to be a vital principle in spiritual warfare. Whenever possible, we should avoid acting alone in such situations: but sometimes spiritual confrontations cannot be avoided. However, even when it seems that no-one else is standing there with us, we can always make a conscious choice to *stay in the shade of his tents*.

This means that, when we become aware that we are facing a spiritual attack, we should concentrate on keeping close to Jesus and staying in the place He has commanded us to be. We do this by being obedient to Him and getting on with the things He has told us to do. This is the place of safety and spiritual rest where, even if things may get a bit hot at times, our enemy cannot harm our spirit or frustrate the purposes of God.

We may still need to explicitly rebuke the enemy in such situations: but only to the extent required for the task in hand. The enemy, for his part, will always try to lure us away from this position, so that we attempt to do more than the Lord has actually told us to do at that time – acting out of unwise zeal or foolish bravado. If he can get us away from that place of obedience and shelter, we will be vulnerable to attack; or if he can distract our attention from the Lord onto his own activities, causing us to fret and worry, he can make us unproductive.

Suppose that a wolf came while the Seeker was feeding her flock. Very likely, on seeing it, she would call out; and the wolf, knowing that it had been rumbled, would be forced to withdraw. But if she stopped what she was doing and went after the wolf, it could turn on her; or lure her away and sneak back to attack the flock. And if she spends too much time watching the wolf, the flock won't get fed!

'I see your Potential' (1:9-11)

I love your spirit (1:9)

⁹I have pictured you, my darling, as a prancing steed in Pharaoh's chariots!

The word translated as 'prancing steed' (AV 'company of horses') is found nowhere else; so its precise meaning is uncertain, though most translators opt for 'mare' or 'filly.' But a strong indication of its significance is given by the word 'horse,' from which it is derived; for in Hebrew this comes from a root meaning, 'a joyfully prancing one.'

Pharaoh's chariots were built for speed, whether in competition or battle. So by combining these two concepts we get a wonderful picture of a high-spirited creature, harnessed to a swift chariot, prancing about and stamping its feet in impatient anticipation of the charge.

To anyone familiar with horses, such a display of spirit is a hallmark of a potential winner. In the same way, the king sees her eagerness to be with him, and is delighted by it. He knows that she has the potential to be the kind of woman who can ravish his heart.

I will make you more beautiful still (1:10-11)

¹⁰Your cheeks are lovely with ear-rings[1], your neck with beads.
¹¹We will make for you ear-rings of gold with studs of silver.

The King loves her beauty: but he won't stop there. He wants to bless her and make her look even more beautiful. She probably has very little jewellery of her own: but that does not matter, because he promises to provide the things she needs.

> Some translations have v.11 by the daughters of Jerusalem: but, as they appear to be speaking of jewellery rather than clothing, it seems more likely that the King is speaking about his craftsmen.

---

[1]   'Ear-rings' translation uncertain. From a root word meaning, 'to explore,' that implies a circular or 'to-and-fro' pattern.

God loves us just as we are now: but He has never finished with us. He, too, is constantly seeking to make us even more beautiful. If we live for Him, our lives will be a constant process of change, steadily becoming more like Him (2 Cor 3:18, 2 Pet 1:5-8, etc.). As with the Seeker, it does not matter that we feel unable to achieve this ourselves: because Jesus has committed Himself and all the resources of his Holy Spirit in order to complete this work in us.

For we are his workmanship, created in Christ Jesus for good works, which God prepared before that we would walk in them. (Eph 2:10)

... being confident of this very thing, that he who began a good work in you will complete it until the day of Jesus Christ. (Phil 1:6)

(See also Ps 138:8)

THE ALLURE OF HIS PRESENCE (1:12-2:7)

Worth more than any treasure (1:12)

¹²While the king is at his table, my spikenard has given out its fragrance.

Spikenard was a very expensive perfume, and this was hers. It would have been a treasured possession of immense value, often handed down through the generations as a family heirloom. It was spikenard, for example, that Mary poured on the head and feet of Jesus (John 12:3-7). That one bottle of Mary's had been worth 300 denarii – about ten month's wages.

This was too valuable to lose, and too valuable to use; like an expensive vintage wine that sits in the wine cellar or passes slowly from dealer to dealer. But how can you ever appreciate its true worth unless it is used? If the stopper is never pulled, the bottle may as well contain water. Indeed, wine that is kept too long may eventually react with the cork and end up tasting foul. So, if it is ultimately to have any proven value, someone must finally summon up the courage to take out the stopper and use it; no matter what the price.

But, like wine, spikenard can be poured out only once. Its odour will linger for a while, and then it is gone, leaving only an evocative memory. So you must be very careful in choosing where and when you will use it. The occasion must justify the sacrifice. By doing this now, she was demonstrating that her desire to please the king and remain in his presence outweighed all other considerations and cautions. She had to have him, whatever the cost.

That is what our Seeker did, and that is what Mary did. What about you? Are you willing to blow your nest-egg, forfeit your security – even risk disappointment and failure – and give up that which is most precious to you, for the sake of your relationship with Jesus?

His presence brings sweet relief (1:13-14)

A bundle of myrrh (1:13)

[13]My beloved is like a bundle of myrrh to me; he shall pass the night between my breasts.

Myrrh was obtained from the bark of a tree similar to an acacia. It was extracted as a sticky resin, which thickened into a gummy substance. In this form, it was of limited use: but by seething in oil, its volatile active ingredients could be absorbed to form Oil of Myrrh or other ointments.

Many of us know myrrh best from its mention in the old carol, 'We Three Kings;' which describes it as a bitter perfume, associated with burial. Indeed, the name actually comes from a root word meaning 'bitter;' and it was used for embalming (e.g. John 19:39); but it was also highly prized for several other purposes.

Its great merit lay in its anti-bacterial, anti-fungal, insect-repellent and odour-suppressing properties. So, besides being used for embalming, it was a very effective ingredient for skin ointments, widely used both for ceremonial purification (as in Ex 30:23-33) and as a healing and beauty treatment. In Esther 2:12, for example, we read that the young women chosen as possible wives for the king were purified for six months with Oil of Myrrh; which would have healed any sores, leaving their skin smooth and supple. We will come across this practice later in the song.

But this particular verse alludes to another use. Women would often wear a small bundle containing myrrh under their clothes. This would probably have had two main functions; as a deodorant and as an insect repellent. Those who have endured long, sultry nights in a hot, sticky climate – pestered by mosquitoes and such-like biting insects – will readily appreciate the sense of delight and relief a bundle of myrrh might bring! She would not readily part with such a treasure.

And, just as the myrrh brought relief from the trials of the climate, so his nearness was a delight to her. Simply having him there, she felt safe, protected from harm – so caught up with him that she forgot about her own difficulties and was at peace.

And what was true of her king is far more true of Jesus. He protects us, cleanses us and blots out the lingering memories of our past failures. In his presence, we forget about ourselves and are overwhelmed by his peace.

But there is a sense of giving on her part here, too. Although I have been a very happily married man for over thirty years, I have never achieved my ambition of spending a whole night in such a position. It's not that my wife doesn't love me, nor that we don't both love to embrace like this – it's just that, well, after a time it gets *uncomfortable* (for both of us, in fact – though I try to avoid admitting this).

So when she pledges to let him sleep all night between her breasts, that's really something!

> Those who are married will understand: but if you are not, think what it's like cuddling a child in your arms as they go to sleep. It's such a great feeling, having that child so trustingly enfolded in your arms, that you hardly dare move for fear of disturbing them. But after a while, the urge to move takes over. You feel the need to restore the circulation to an arm or leg, and you begin to discreetly change position.
>
> Eventually, you find a way of extricating yourself and laying them down to sleep in peace.

Only if we are absolutely dedicated will we sacrifice our urge to move for the sake of being so close to the one we love.

When we come into times of deep intimacy with Jesus, we need to guard them well: for surely the urge to move will grip us. I am finding that to be still before God, simply keeping my attention firmly on Him, is one of the most difficult spiritual disciplines of them all. We are unaccustomed to being still in his presence. Like Peter on the mount of transfiguration, we feel an uncontrollable urge to say or do something. Or, as the disciples in Gethsemane, we may simply let our thoughts drift and fall asleep.

I am not speaking of a 'Christianised' form of transcendental meditation here. The eastern mystic seeks to empty their mind of thoughts: but in the presence of Jesus, the mind is **preoccupied** with Him; just as her mind would have been flooded with thoughts of her lover. It is from this deep and powerful sense of fulfilment and utter satisfaction that the desire for stillness flows. It is immensely potent: it changes our priorities, our whole outlook on life – even our everyday behaviour, for as long as we keep our desire focussed on Him.

For this reason the spiritual powers of world darkness, who see in our intimacy with Jesus the greatest possible threat to their own power, will do all they can to disrupt and minimize our enjoyment of such times. This will take various forms, ranging from external interruptions through to direct spiritual attack. But often the greatest threat is our own human nature, that does not readily give up its natural impulses to anyone, and constantly wants its own way. (Indeed, when we suffer interruptions, we must always take care that we handle these with grace, or our own impatience will cause more discord than the event that provoked it.)

The secret of Engedi (1:14)

[14]*As a cluster of henna blossom in the vineyards of Engedi is my beloved to me!*

Most scholars now agree that the Hebrew word *'kopher'* (translated 'Camphire' in the AV) refers to the blossom of the Henna plant. Henna was a highly-prized perfume and skin colouring, having a sweet smell and producing red or yellow tones that were considered to be the height of fashion. It was rare and valuable, having to be imported from distant lands at great cost. Few of the ladies of Jerusalem would ever have seen it except in its dried form. It is said that they would perfume themselves by crushing the dried flowers in their hands and rubbing them over their breasts.

But now let me tell you about Engedi. It is situated in one of the most inhospitable places on earth, in the wilderness along the western shore of the Dead Sea. It lies along an ancient caravan route: but one used as little as possible because it was so arduous. The Dead Sea depression is the lowest place on earth, and one of the hottest. To make matters worse, those who travelled by its shores were constantly tormented by its sparkling waters; which were a constant reminder of their thirst – and yet death to drink. (The water is ten times saltier than the sea; and nothing lives in it). Along the entire 50 miles of that terrible coast there are just two places where fresh water can be found: the springs of Ein Feshka, at the northern end, and Engedi ('The Fountain of the Kid'), about half-way along its length.

Imagine yourself as a lady travelling in a caravan from Jerusalem along that dreadful route. Few of her peers would ever have been that way. The heat is suffocating, the sun blistering and relentless, and the smell of stale sweat everywhere. There is nothing to be seen but dust, bare rock, the white glint of salt and that deadly, mocking water. Few natural places come closer to a description of 'hell on earth' than this.

Finally, after excruciating hours of discomfort, this barren landscape is broken by the wondrous sight of a streak of luxuriant green! From the spring of Engedi, in a gorge 600 feet (200m) above the valley floor, a stream of fresh water flows, bringing life to this place of death. There are even vineyards! How the travellers would have hurried to reach that place, and rest among the cool of the vines!

No doubt our lady would have hoped that, just possibly, she might find a fresh, sweet bunch of grapes awaiting her: but what she actually found would have taken her breath away. Here, in this terrible wilderness, is a sight and fragrance she has only ever known before as a distant dream, faded and dry, though still heart-rendingly sweet. Yet here is the reality – wild henna, in full bloom! For, even to this day, Engedi is the *only* place it grows in all Israel.

Can you imagine the sense of wonder and delight she would have felt as, after all those hours of torment, for the first time in her life she pressed this sweetest and most precious of blooms against her breast; as she smelt its rich, fresh, potent perfume and wondered at the vibrant colour of the marks on her skin? Is it any exaggeration to say that her 'hell on earth' has suddenly become a 'heaven on earth'?

This, then, is the image our Seeker uses to describe what her king means to her. Before she met him, her life was a barren wilderness: but now, suddenly, it is a paradise of delight.

How much more will those of us who have met with Jesus recognise in this a picture of that first meeting! Until then, life was an existence, frequently a hard struggle, interspersed with occasional hints that, somehow, somewhere, there must be something better. We would catch glimpses of truth, love and beauty: but always they seemed faded and flawed; and we would wonder whether there really was a perfect original, or whether the cynics were right who said life was just an illusion.

And then, when such hopes seemed pointless, and often when things were at their very worst and we least expected it, suddenly Jesus came into our lives. Here was truth in all its beauty and love in all its tenderness! Now we know our hope is real!

So what if there are still miles of wilderness left to cross? Now she can face whatever obstacles remain, for she will take this precious fragrance with her; just as He will remain with us to support us in all that lies ahead, no matter what that may be.

Drawn by her gaze (1:15)

[15]*How fair you are, my darling; how fair you are! Your eyes are like doves.'*

The words 'my darling,' and 'dove' are typically used by the king, when addressing the Seeker. It is not just that she is delighted with him: he is delighted by her beauty, and he wants her to know it.

But it is her eyes that command his attention.

A dove's eyes are widely spaced, and when it looks at you, they stand out; giving it an expression of wide-eyed wonder and guileless innocence. No doubt she, too, is gazing at him, and the expression in her eyes is saying 'I love you. You amaze me. I am yours, with no preconditions and no reservations.'

As we progress through this song, we will see how deeply affected the king is by the way she looks at him. Love evokes love; and love reciprocated evokes yet more.

The same is true of our relationship with God. When God looks on us, to find us quietly gazing back at Him, it thrills his heart, and our spiritual eyes lock on one another in moments of deep intimacy.

It has been said that there is nothing I can do that will make God love me any less, and nothing that I can do that will make Him love me any more. In one sense, that is absolutely true: for God's love is totally unconditional, and based solely on what He has done for us: not on the little that we can do for Him. Yet there is also a sense in which it is *not* true, and there *is* something that we can do. It is a matter of potential and fulfilment, of yearning and satisfaction.

Take the prodigal son, for example (Luke 15:11-32). During the time that he was away from home, the heart of his father yearned for him; even though, apparently, reports of his son's riotous and immoral behaviour had from time to time reached him (see v.30). Arguably, the love that remains steadfast in the face of such disappointment and provocation is at least as great, if not greater, than that which is lavished on the son when he is at home. Yet which brings the greater delight?

Without a doubt, it is when father and son look into one another's eyes, and the father says, 'I love you, Son,' and the son hugs him and answers, 'I know, Dad, and I love you, too.' But this is not greater love on the father's part: *it is love fulfilled.*

God just loves it when we look at Him that way!

What do surroundings matter? (1:16-17)

[16]How fair you are, my beloved; delightful indeed! And our couch is green.
[17]The beams of our house are cedars; our rafters – firs.

The Seeker echoes back the Kings compliment. We can tell this is her speaking because, although the Hebrew word 'fair' may be applied equally to men and women, the word translated as 'beloved' here and elsewhere is a predominantly masculine term, used throughout the song to refer to the King.

'Beloved' is actually one of those curious words with several quite distinct meanings. We have already seen another of these: used as an abstract plural, it is translated as 'love' or 'lovings' in 1:2, 1:4, 4:10 and 7:12. Its other use is as the standard Hebrew word for 'uncle.' Thus, the word has associations not only of sexual attraction, but also of a very deep, practical, caring love.

> In Hebrew society, the husband's brother was the 'nearest kinsman' – next in importance to the husband himself.
>
> If the husband died, the brother was expected to care for the family. Indeed, if the widow were childless, he was even expected to marry her; so she could have children to inherit her dead husband's name and wealth.

But now the question arises, 'Where are they?'

The most obvious answer seems to be, 'In a house.' But what is the significance of the colour of their couch, or the kind of wood used for the roof? The word translated 'green' is actually a term signifying freshness and new growth, rather than simply colour. So perhaps, bearing in mind the king's love of the outdoors, they are comparing their couch and ceiling to the fresh grass and trees of the forest.

But then, another possibility comes to mind. What if they are actually lying in a forest glade and, in effect, saying that the grass and the trees are just as good as any palace?

That there is a comparison being made seems probable: but, as to which way round it is, we cannot really tell. So maybe the key point here is that, when they are in each other's arms, it really doesn't matter where they are: a forest glade will feel like a palace, and a room like the great outdoors. They would be just as happy, and feel just as rich, in either.

As the old song goes, 'What matters where on earth we dwell, on mountain top, or in the dell, in cottage or in mansion fair? Where Jesus is, it's heaven there!'

He only has eyes for you (2:1-2)

[1]*I am a rose of Sharon, a lily of the valleys.*
[2]*As a lily among thorns, so is my darling among the daughters.*

'Rose of Sharon' has such a lovely sound and association for western minds that many have applied it to Jesus, deducing that this must be the King speaking. But, while there is some debate as to its correct botanical identification[1], virtually all suggestions point – not to a very large, solitary flower like a rose, but – to low-growing flowers that appear in large masses. This would mean that, to an observer, no one flower stands out significantly from the thousands, or even millions, of others. And this was even more true of the lilies which, though strikingly beautiful, grew like grass in the fields (see Luke 12:27-28).

This means it is more probable that verse 1 is spoken by the Seeker. She has been despised by her family, and has a low opinion of herself. So now, confronted with the love of the king, she cannot grasp just how special she is to him, and says, in effect, 'I know he says I'm beautiful: but I'm really just one among thousands.'

But the king won't accept this. He replies, 'To me you stand out like a lily surrounded by thorns.' When he looks at her, he sees only her; and all else seems insignificant or even ugly by

---

[1]   Possible identifications of the rose of Sharon are: **Anenome** (*anenome fulgens*), 10-30cm high, spring / early summer flowers, 5-7cm, red with 10-15 petals; **Autumn Crocus / Meadow Saffron** (*colchicum autumnale*), autumn flowers 13-18 cm high, 5-8cm across, pink / lavender with 6 petals forming a cup; **Rock Rose** (*cistus*, 4 possible species) forms clumps up to 75cm, spring / early summer flowers, 4-5cm, pink / purple / lilac with 5 petals like tissue paper; **Narcissus** (*narcissus tazetta*) 30-45cm high, spring flowers, 2-4cm, 6 white / cream petals with a yellow cup.

comparison. Even amongst the daughters of Jerusalem, many of whom were no doubt very attractive, she holds his gaze to the exclusion of all others.

We know that Jesus loves us all: but the amazing thing is that, whenever we come to Him, His love is so personal and intimate that it is as if there is no-one else in the world but Him and you!

This is the ideal of love that Solomon was trying to expound; though, of course, for him it was impossible. He was a mere man, with only so much love, time and attention to give. Whatever he gave to one inevitably meant he had that much less for another: and that didn't just affect his relationship with his wives, but his relationship with God as well.

But God, being infinite and unlimited in his love and his very nature, can do what Solomon couldn't. He can give to each one of us all the love and attention we could possibly wish for, and yet still leave his vast reserves undiminished.

How can I illustrate this?

As a computer programmer, I sometimes compare it to connecting my own little desktop computer to a huge super computer – one so powerful that no request for information or assistance ever fails to return an instant response, even though it is simultaneously talking to hundreds of other computers like my own. For each computer, it seems as if it has the super computer's undivided attention.

But that is a rather cold and clinical comparison. It is not just a matter of sheer power – we are also dealing here with the timelessness of God. Imagine someone stooping for a whole hour to gaze at a single flower in a field. But when he has finished, instead of walking on, he stoops to gaze for another hour at the flower next to it; and the same for the next, and the next... until he has gone over the entire field! Even with so many millions of people in the world, God is never in a hurry. He is the God of eternity, existing above and beyond time as we know it; so He always has time to take such a personal interest in us that, for us, it is as if there was no-one else.

One passage of scripture illustrates this for me more vividly than any other, even though I often refer to it as, 'the most boring chapter in the Bible.' It is Numbers 7:10-88; and it describes the offerings made over a 12-day period for the dedication of the tabernacle. Don't worry, I won't quote the whole thing: but here's a taster:

> He who offered his offering the first day was Nahshon the son of Amminadab, of the tribe of Judah, and his offering was: one silver platter, the weight of which was one hundred thirty shekels, one silver bowl of seventy shekels, after the shekel of the sanctuary; both of them full of fine flour mixed with oil for a meal offering; one golden ladle of ten shekels, full of incense; one young bull, one ram, one male lamb a year old, for a burnt offering; one male goat for a sin offering; and for the sacrifice of peace offerings, two head of cattle, five rams, five male goats, and five male lambs a year old. This was the offering of Nahshon the son of Amminadab.
>
> (Num 7:12-17.)

The poor scribe who had to copy this out by hand (and then count every letter to make sure nothing had been missed) may have wondered why it was necessary to describe the offering in such tedious detail! But then he would come to day 2: and, lo and behold, here is another equally detailed description of that day's offering; then on day 3 the same. And by then the realisation would be dawning on this hapless scribe; all these offerings are not simply much the same as one another – they are identical! The only thing that changes is the number of the day and the name of the man making the offering. And there are still another 9 days to go… He must have almost screamed, 'Why, oh why, didn't he just say, "Ditto"?!'

But all scripture is given for our instruction: and that is exactly the point; *God NEVER says, 'Ditto,' when we come to worship Him*. We may listen to others pray, and then think to ourselves, 'What's left for me to bring? It's all been said already.' But God is like that man looking at the flowers in the field. He is passionately interested in even the tiniest details of your relationship; and it doesn't matter to Him whether what you bring is different from anyone else's offering or not. This is you and your love: and to Him that makes it utterly unique and special. For Him, as well as you, it is as if no one else is even there.

As Psalm 139 says, 'Where shall I flee from your presence?' He gives us all the attention we can possibly handle and more – we are so utterly surrounded by his presence that it is as if we are swimming in it! Everywhere we go, we find his gaze is on us – a keen, passionate, personal gaze that knows and loves us better than we do ourselves.

Overwhelmed by his love (2:3-5)

³*As an apricot¹ tree among the trees of the wood, so is my beloved among the sons. I have dwelt in his shade with great delight, and his fruit is sweet to my mouth.*
⁴*He brought me into the banqueting house, and his banner over me was love.*
⁵*Refresh me with raisin-cakes, strengthen me with apricots! For I am weak with love.*

Hearing him declare just how special she is to him, she responds with a similar analogy. Few woodland trees were noted for succulent fruits: but apricots were. So she conjures up this image of wandering, tired and hungry, through a wood, and her delight at finding this tree. Surrounded by trees, this one tree holds her gaze; for in it she finds all she craves for: beauty, rest, shelter and refreshment.

In modern Hebrew 'tappuach,' like 'tuffach' in Arabic, means 'apple:' but scholars question its earlier meaning. Israel's hot, dry climate did not favour apples, so they were mostly low quality: whereas here, and in Joel 1:12, tappuach is ranked among their most prized fruits.

I therefore side with those who translate this as 'apricot.' These were cultivated in Persia since ancient times and thrive in Israel. They are beautiful to look at, provide thick shade, and their fruit is both sweet and fragrant.

---

¹ "The corresponding Arabic word, *tyffach*, signifies not only *apples* but also generally all similar fruits, such as oranges, lemons, quinces, peaches, apricots, etc." *Calmet's Dictionary of the Holy Bible*, Augustin Calmet, Charles Taylor – 1830.

But, she says, he didn't stop there. He took her into his banqueting house. The Hebrew words literally mean 'the house of wine.' In Hebrew thinking, wine was seen as bringing 'gladness of heart' (see Ps 104:15). So the thought conveyed here is not simply that there is an abundance of food and drink: but that she has been released from feelings of sorrow and emptiness and is now free to be truly happy.

Yet it is neither food nor wine that crowns this occasion for her.

High, above all, plain for all to see – but especially for her – is a banner, his banner, carrying a single word that says it all: 'Love.'

All that he does for her, he does for love. All that he will be for her, he will be because of love. And the most precious thing he can ever give to her is not the pageantry, or the provision, but the passion of their love for one another.

I mentioned before that I began my study using a Russian bible; and the way it translates '*weak*' in verse 5 is so apt. It uses a word that conveys the idea, 'I am not just incapable: I am way out beyond the limits of my own capability.' And it's all because of love. Her desire for him has become so deep, so intense, that it has consumed all her energy; until she is, quite literally, afraid that she is going to faint. Hence the cry for raisins and apricots, which are a rich source of natural sugars. Although they would not have known the science, they were clearly familiar with their restorative value in such situations.

The combined picture is of a love that is utterly over whelming in the intensity of its passion; intense in his passion for her, and overwhelming in the response it evokes from her. She is stirred to the point where she is beyond strength and has nothing left to give; and yet still knows that she has given nowhere near enough.

Again, it is like that for us with Jesus. Perhaps mercifully for us, most of the time we simply fail to grasp the sheer immensity of his love. We acknowledge it as an intellectual truth; yet it is so far beyond the power of our minds to truly comprehend, that it remains a somewhat abstract concept to us.

It is like our concept of infinity. We know what it means in theory: but then there are those moments when we are confronted by the sheer immensity of the universe we live in, and are shocked into awe. In the same way, as you come to know Jesus, there are moments when God grants you a flash of insight into the depth and height of the love He has for you; and the effect leaves you emotionally stunned.

In his arms (2:6-7)

6His left hand is under my head, and his right hand embraces me.
7I have charged you, O daughters of Jerusalem, by the gazelles, and by the hinds of the field: do not awaken or stir up love until it desires.

Some commentators see these verses as meaning that he is asleep, with her in his arms. But, if you think about it, this would not have been a very comfortable sleeping position!

It is more consistent with him either lying above or beside her, propped up on his elbow, or else embracing her while they are standing. The hand behind her head suggests they are face to face, kissing or gazing into each other's eyes.

> I recall reading one author who saw v.6 as a reference to sexual foreplay: but I think that is too fanciful. Both text and context imply their relationship is not yet at that stage.
>
> Firstly, 'embrace' means just that: it's the Hebrew word used to describe how a man greets a close relative or a woman holds a baby.
>
> Secondly, their wedding is described in the next chapter: and the Old Testament law treats extra-marital sex as a very serious offence. The penalty was obligatory marriage, with no right to divorce, and a massive compensation payment of fifty pieces of silver (Deut 22:28-29).

She then gives us a rather enigmatic charge (or command) not to 'awaken or stir up love until it desires' – one that is repeated twice more, in 3:5 and 8:5. Some translations render this as 'stir not up nor awaken *my* love until *he* pleases,' building on the idea that he is asleep. But the Hebrew for 'love' here is the same as that used in verses 4 and 5, where it plainly means love itself, rather than the one who is loved. In fact, it occurs some 40 times in the Old Testament; and on every occasion it refers to love itself rather than a person.

So what do these mysterious words mean? We are being warned that love should not be aroused too soon: but why, and how this might happen, is not explained.

We will consider this further later.

THE CHALLENGE OF THE BEYOND (2:8-3:5)

Lord of the mountains (2:8-9)

⁸The voice of my beloved! Look, he comes leaping over the mountains, skipping upon the hills. ⁹My beloved is like a gazelle or a young hart. See! he stands behind our wall, gazing at the windows, peering through the lattice.

Initially, the Seeker is delighted with the outgoing spirit of her shepherd King.

Here is someone who does not hide away in a comfortable palace. He will not accept any 'no-go' areas in any part of his domain: but will visit them all and rule over them all. He even makes mountains look easy! He is strong and agile. It seems that nothing is too hard for him and nothing can daunt or stop him.

But alongside this she now knows that, despite everything he has 'out there,' he is still passionately drawn to her. To see him coming back from such faraway places, yet so evidently longing to see her again, reinforces all he has told her about how precious she is to him. For perhaps the first time in her life, she really feels she is worth something – in fact, that she is worth more to her king than anything else in his kingdom!

Security and the knowledge that we are loved are two of our deepest human needs. Formerly, she enjoyed neither. She felt she was of no real value. And who would bother to care for her, when even her own family was against her? But how dramatically and completely her circumstances have been transformed! Seeing his ability to cope with every situation she need never feel insecure again: and with his passion for her, she need never feel worthless again.

It's the same for us, only more so, when we come to know Jesus. Even kings have limits to their power and possessions: but He has none. Yet his love for us is so great that He was willing to leave heaven and accept death on a cross to win us to Himself. Such love is the guarantee of our security and personal value, no matter what trials may come our way. As Paul wrote, 'If God is for us, who can be against us?

> *What then shall we say about these things? If God is for us, who can be against us? He who didn't spare his own Son, but delivered him up for us all, how would he not also with him freely give us all things? Who could bring a charge against God's chosen ones? It is God who justifies. Who is he who condemns? It is Christ who died, yes rather, who was raised from the dead, who is at the right hand of God, who also makes intercession for us.*
>
> *Who shall separate us from the love of Christ? Could oppression, or anguish, or persecution, or famine, or nakedness, or peril, or sword? Even as it is written, "For your sake we are killed all day long. We were accounted as sheep for the slaughter". No, in all these things, we are more than conquerors through him who loved us. For I am persuaded, that neither death, nor life, nor angels, nor principalities, nor things present, nor things to come, nor powers, nor height, nor depth, nor any other created thing, will be able to separate us from the love of God, which is in Christ Jesus our Lord*
>
> (Rom 8:31-39)

Come with me (2:10-13)

[10]*My beloved answered, and said to me, "Rise up, my darling, my fair one, and come away.* [11]*For – see! – the winter is past. The rain is over – it's gone!* [12]*The flowers are seen on the land; the time of song has come, and the call of the turtledove has been heard in our land.* [13]*The fig tree ripens her early figs, and the vines are fragrant with blossoms. Rise up, my darling, my fair one, and come away!"*

But now here comes the catch – and it's a very big catch. *The king wants her to go with him!*

You may think, 'Wonderful! Why not?' But remember he has just come from the mountains. In those days these were *really* wild places, frequented by dangerous carnivores, bandits and other hazards; and there were no comfortable tourist centres, or even camp sites, for nature-lovers. Most 'sensible,' 'civilised' people kept as far away from such places as possible.

She is mostly accustomed to tending vineyards. Foxes were the biggest carnivores she normally had to worry about. And after the emotional battering she has had over the past years, her self-confidence is still at a pretty low ebb.

She knows that, even with his help and protection, the conditions out there will be difficult for her; and she doesn't think she can cope. This certainly does *not* sound like a good idea to her!

But he wants to share his life and his loves with her. He wants them to be one. So he tries to reassure her and tell her about some of the beautiful things he wants to show her. The weather is good; it's springtime – the season of new beginnings. Everything will be at its freshest and best. It will be wonderful, he says, and we can enjoy it all together.

Sadly, she is not convinced.

We, too, tend to react in the same way when Jesus begins to really start sharing his heart with us.

He is the Shepherd King, always the Shepherd King, and his heart constantly yearns and aches for the lost, the dying, the unwanted, the far away… He longs to be one with us: but that is only truly possible as we learn to understand how He feels, and begin to share that passion.

But it's a dangerous and uncomfortable place to be; so, when He begins asking us to go with Him into difficult situations, we back away. We would rather admire the immensity of his love from a safe distance; because our fearful hearts tell us that we could never cope with the demands it will place upon us.

Don't hide away (2:14-15)

[14]*My dove, in the clefts of the crag, in the cover of the steep place, let me look upon your appearance, let me hear your voice; for your voice is sweet and your appearance lovely.*

[15]*Let us catch the foxes, the little foxes that destroy the vineyards – our vineyards, which are in blossom.*

She continues to shrink back, like a bird hiding itself among the rocks.

He seeks to coax her out to join him by reminding her of his love for her. But, getting no response, he changes tack slightly, reminding her of a problem with which she is more familiar...

To most people, there is no obvious reason why foxes, which mostly eat meat, should be a problem in a vineyard. But for a Hebrew, the explanation is found in the name itself – it means a 'burrower.' The vine terraces were built up with the finest quality soil heaped around the vine roots. From the foxes' point of view, this was prime real estate – ideal for digging their burrows, plus the added bonus of all that lovely shelter provided by the spreading leaves! But their digging would tear away at the vine's roots. **No root means no fruit**: so the little burrowers had to be stopped. Otherwise, the crop would be ruined.

By reminding her of this, he was offering her a challenge that was within the realm of her own experience and capability; and at the same time he was making an important point. Just as the vines needed to be rooted in the soil to be fruitful, so her confidence needed to be rooted in him. Her doubts and fears were like the foxes, undermining her relationship with him, and preventing her from becoming all she was meant to be.

Without the King, it is undoubtedly true that she could not have handled the challenge of the call out into the wild country. No more can we cope with the immensity of the needs and challenges in this world in which we live: and for the most part our strategy is just like hers – we try to hide away from it, restricting our lives to those areas where we feel secure. But we need to understand two vital things here. Firstly, He is not asking us to face this alone; and, secondly, He understands our weaknesses and will tailor the challenge to our current experience and ability. So we need to get our eyes off our own inadequacies and fixed again on the all-sufficiency and faithfulness of the One who is our lover, guide and protector.

If we learn to trust and obey his leading and rely upon the support that He provides, then nothing that He asks us to do will ever be impossible to us. But if we allow doubt and fear to undermine our relationship with Jesus it will prevent us from growing into the kind of people He wants us to be. The result will be a life that fails to produce the kind of results He knows we are capable of. For in the spiritual realm the same law applies: *no root means no fruit.*

Incremental Faith

The king knows the Seeker is not ready for the challenge of the mountains. In fact, he never even suggests it at this stage; though she has rightly guessed that this is where his invitation will ultimately lead.

But he is not asking this of her. He asks only that she be willing to go with him to the limits of her present confidence, and then allows him to lead her gently into the territory that lies just beyond.

This is how faith grows. There is no need to berate ourselves over our 'lack of faith,' nor screw ourselves up to perform some heroic 'act of faith' that we have not yet been asked to do. All we have to do is openly acknowledge our doubts and fears, and then take the next step that is asked of us.

Faith for what follows will come in its own due time.

I didn't hear that... (2:16-17)

[16]*My beloved is mine, and I am his: he grazes (his flock) among the lilies.*

[17]*Until the day dawns, and the shadows flee – turn, my beloved, and be like a gazelle or a young hart on the cloven[1] mountains.*

---

[1] The Hebrew, '*Bether,*' means 'cut in pieces.'

She responds by telling us how confident she is of the king's love and that she, for her part, is sold out to him. She tells us that he is off to graze his flock among the lilies. Then she turns and bids him go and have a good night out in the mountains.

Yet, all the time, we know full well that he is actually standing a little way off begging her to come with him: and she won't.

This is unreality.

She is not yet as confident of his love for her, nor as committed in her love for him, as she claims to be; or she would be going with him. But, because she is afraid to face the challenge, or face up honestly to her fear, she resorts to superficial professions of love while she pretends not to have heard or understood what he is saying to her.

Sadly, we do not have to look far in our own lives, nor in the present day church in general, to find countless examples of the same kind of spiritual unreality. We love to sing hymns saying how much we love Jesus and what a powerful and loving friend He is. But when He challenges us to move out of our comfort zones we start suffering from hearing loss, or a sudden lack of comprehension.

If only we would at least be honest about it and say, 'Yes, I know I should come with You; but I'm afraid. I don't think I can let go of my security yet.' If she had spoken to him of her fears then, doubtless, he could have given her more reassurances, and led her by gentle degrees from dealing with foxes to facing down lions. But by pretending as she does, she will leave him no choice but to withdraw; since to impose his will on her would undermine the spontaneous, voluntary love he wants her to enjoy.

In the same way, when we try to cover our fear and unwillingness with exaggerated professions of love it may sound very spiritual; but our unreality actually obstructs God's work in our lives. We can never fool Him when we try to conceal our reservations and avoid the things He is saying. Rather, to Him they spell out in big, bold letters, "THIS

SUBJECT IS NOT UP FOR DISCUSSION JUST NOW. PLEASE PRETEND THAT YOU HAVEN'T NOTICED".

Don't get me wrong here. I am not talking about the very commendable practice of regularly declaring out the truth about God's love for us, our standing in Him, the love that we do genuinely feel for Him and the greater love that we aspire to – even though in our hearts we know that our love is really so inadequate. This is one of the best possible ways of building up our faith and confidence in Him. What I am talking about is the way we sometimes use truth to camouflage our real feelings.

We may be saying exactly the same things, just as the things she says here sound very little different from what she has said before: but there is a subtle shift in our motives, and it is that motivation, rather than what is actually said, that is critical.

Are you pressing closer, or backing away? Previously, she was constantly seeking ways of getting closer to her king, even begging to be allowed to go out shepherding with him. But now he is urging her to come, and she is pretending not to hear.

Her last words to the king show another of our 'defence mechanisms' in action – *leave it till tomorrow.* 'You go and do it,' she says, 'I'll see you in the morning.'

I recall once hearing an imaginary tale of three demons being interviewed by Satan for the post of Chief Tempter. To each of them, Satan put the question, 'What would be your recommended strategy to keep mankind from turning to God?'

One advocated promoting all kinds of self-indulgence. The next suggested filling the world with suffering and violence until men cursed the very notion of a loving God.

But the one who got the job simply said, 'I would tell them, "You can think about God later. There's plenty of time…" '

We may or may not get more time tomorrow, but one thing is certain: whatever time we do not spend following God now is lost time – time spent in disobedience, out of touch with Him. The sooner we deal with our reservations, the better.

The Loneliness of Disobedience (3:1)

¹On my bed, in the night, I had looked for the one my soul loves. I looked for him: but did not find him.

The king takes her at her word, and leaves. For a while, perhaps, she feels relieved that he did not press her to go with him.

But soon she begins to feel an aching loneliness. In her fear of the unknown, she had forgotten just how precious he has become to her. But now she is alone again she realises afresh that, for her, there is only one thing that can satisfy; and that is to be with her king.

If only he would come back! Perhaps then, they could spend some more time together. Maybe, eventually, she might pluck up the courage to go with him; or maybe, if she begged him, he might change his mind and spend the night there with her. She lies on her bed, unable to sleep, imagining that each sound she hears might be his returning footsteps, or his voice in the distance. But there is no further voice, and he does not come.

Longing alone is not enough: she cannot find him by remaining where she is.

There is a vital principle we need to understand here. If we refuse to listen to God's voice, He will not multiply disobedience in our lives by repeatedly urging us, or asking us to do other things. He does not withdraw his love: but, like her lover, He withdraws his presence, and there is silence. And if there is a genuine flame of love in our hearts then, like her, we will begin to miss Him, and long for a renewing of the intimacy we have lost.

Let me unpack that a bit. Every time God asks us to do something, and we don't, then we are hardening our hearts towards Him: and that is not a good state to be in. We are establishing no-go areas in our lives, while our consciences become callused and less sensitive to God. This is the exact opposite of what He is seeking to accomplish. His desire is for ever-increasing intimacy and sensitivity towards each other.

The reality is that, when we first come to Jesus, we have a great many problem areas in our lives – so many, in fact, that if God gave us a list of them all at the outset, we simply could not cope. For one thing, we would feel utterly condemned and worthless; for another, we just wouldn't know where to start.

Instead, if we will only let Him, God will set his own priorities in our relationship. Because no two of us are alike, or have the same background, his methods are never exactly the same for any two of us. But the principles on which He operates remain consistent.

He will challenge us to do something that touches one of our problem areas. Like the Seeker, our instinct is often to recoil, and tell ourselves, 'I couldn't possibly do that. He can't really be asking that of me.' (I have complained several times to the Lord that I think He is expressing much too high an opinion of me by the things that He asks!) But He knows what He is doing – and exactly what we are capable of doing, if we will just obey Him. The mere fact that He is asking is his personal guarantee that He will help us to achieve it (1 Cor 10:13).

So if we try to ignore God when He speaks to us like this, we erect a roadblock against the very issue He has judged to be the most appropriate one to deal with right now. We might like to side-step it and move on to something else: but that will leave it more of a problem area than it was before, and establish a pattern of behaviour that makes it harder for us to respond rightly in the future. So God won't do that. Instead, He withdraws and waits.

That is when the loneliness starts to set in.

Jesus said, 'If a man loves me, he will keep my word. My Father will love him, and we will come to him, and make our home with him.' (Jn 14:23.) The flip side of this is that, if you do not keep his word, you will not experience that kind of intimacy.

You may not notice it at first: but, if your heart is still set on knowing God, it won't be long before you begin to realise that something is wrong. You aren't sensing that close presence of his the way you used to; you find you are not experiencing Him speaking directly to your heart the way you used to.

> If you exercise prophetic or other spiritual gifts, don't fall into the trap of thinking they are a proof of your own good standing with God. Rom 11:29 says the gifts of God are without repentance. That is because they are given for the sake of others, rather than you.
>
> It is possible for someone whose life is not right with God to still hear from God to the extent of being able to receive something for others, whilst having lost their own intimacy with God and no longer hearing his will for their own lives. Consider Balaam (Num 22-24). He brought amazing prophecies of God for Israel: but when it came to his own life, his donkey could see things more clearly than he did!
>
> See also Jesus' own warning about this matter in Matt 7:22.

You will begin to hunger for what you have lost, even as you struggle to understand what has gone wrong and why you feel so uneasy and dissatisfied inside. You are starting to feel the loneliness of disobedience.

This loneliness is not pleasant: but it is one of God's greatest kindnesses to us. Rather than compel us to obey, overwhelming us with the realisation of his awesome power and holiness, He waits until we realise for ourselves that it is really Him that we are missing; and that his presence is worth more to us than the comfort of those things that were the original cause of our dis obedience.

It is a risky strategy, to be sure. The father had to watch the prodigal son leave, and wait for him to come to his senses. Many Christians also are seduced into thinking that intimacy with God isn't really all that special; and they settle

N.B. *Times of loneliness are not always our fault.* God sometimes allows such seasons in our lives to refine our character, as with Jesus in the wilderness. And sometimes an overwhelming sense of loneliness can come from sickness, depression or spiritual attack.

If in doubt, ask God sincerely to show you if you have offended or disobeyed Him. If He shows you something specific, deal with it: but if all you have are vague, undefined feelings of guilt or unwor thiness reject them; that is the work of Satan, the Accuser. The Holy Spirit convicts us to cleanse and restore: not to condemn.

down into a lifestyle that pays lip-service to God, whilst lacking the passion of a heart inspired by his love and presence.

Had our Seeker not acted as she does next, she too could well have ended up like many another failed queen: living in the palace but disconnected from her king. Please, please, don't let this happen to you.

Renewing our first love (3:2-5)

Rediscovering the place of obedience (3:2-4a)

²*I will rise now, and go around the city. In the streets and open places I will look for the one my soul loves. I looked for him: but did not find him.*

³*The watchmen that patrol the city found me; to whom I said, "Have you seen the one my soul loves?"*

⁴⁽ᵃ⁾*I had scarcely passed them by when I found the one my soul loves:*
…

Eventually, our Seeker realises that simply lying there waiting isn't going to achieve anything. The king had asked her to go with him, and she has not responded; so now it is up to her to make the next move. So she goes out and starts looking for him.

But though she scours the city streets and squares, her search is fruitless. There seems to be no sign of him. So why is this? It is because he had called her to go with him **beyond** the city walls. Partial obedience is not enough: she needs to do what was originally asked of her.

However, the king doesn't want this to be any harder for her than absolutely necessary. The city walls mark the limit of the area patrolled by the night watchmen. Within those limits her enquiries find no answer. But when she finally summons up the courage to go beyond them, outside the city, then, '*Scarcely had I passed them when I found the one my heart loves.*' Rather than going off on his own, he has either returned or waited for her, believing that she would come; and no sooner does she respond than he is there.

If we have lost our closeness to the Lord, then the best place to find it again is where He last asked us to be.

Often, we look for Him in the place where He last spoke to us (in her case, the bedroom) or, failing that, then we try to meet Him part way, in an area where we still feel comfortable (the city streets). Neither of these will do. The issue here is that we are not hearing his voice because we *refused* to hear it. So to hear Him again we need to reverse that process by moving back into the place of obedience and doing the thing that He asked us to do.

You may be tempted to ask yourself, 'But surely He is so loving that, if I decide I cannot face the issue this time, then He will give me another chance later, when I am more ready for it, won't He?'

That is often true; though not always – and it could take a long time. But, meanwhile, a precious opportunity may have been irretrievably lost; and we can never truly experience the intimacy and inward spiritual release that He wants to give us until we learn to respond to his call.

Notice also that it was more difficult for the Seeker to go outside the city afterwards than it would have been if she had responded when first asked. Then, she would have always been in the company of her king: but afterwards she had to face that challenge alone. The children of Israel were afraid to enter the Promised Land when God first told them to do so. Most of the adults never got a second chance: but those who finally entered only did so after 40 years hardship in the desert.

God always chooses the best time and the best way for us, even if it doesn't always seem that way to us. Prevaricating, once He has made his will clear, never makes the task easier. The safest and easiest way, no matter how risky it may seem to us, is the path of prompt obedience.

But as soon as we finally step back into the realm of committed obedience to his voice, He is there to lead us on. Because, like her king, He has no desire to make our obedience any harder, or to withdraw his presence for any longer, than is absolutely necessary. He longs for fellowship with us far more earnestly than we long for Him.

It is so important that you understand this; because, when we have been through such a time of separation, we may be expecting our relationship to remain strained for some time afterwards. Partly, we feel that we deserve it and, partly, we are unconsciously supposing that He is like some of the people we know, who don't readily forget our faults. We think we will have to suffer in silence for a while and then worm our way back into his favour.

> *We are often slower to forgive ourselves than He is;* so our wounded feelings may take a little time to heal before we feel as confident and assured in his love as we were before. But if we let ourselves be persuaded that He hasn't really forgiven us, then we are being deluded into doubting his character. And such a seed of mistrust can then become the cause of a deeper and more serious rift between us, as we shall see later.

But our King is the source of all grace, mercy, love and forgiveness! He does not deal with us like that! Like the father waiting for the return of the prodigal (Lk 15:20), who *'ran and fell on his neck and kissed him,'* all He waits for is for us to turn back in repentance and open ourselves to his love again.

A deeper commitment (3:4b)

[4(b)] ... I seized him, and would not let him go until I had brought him into my mother's house, into the inner chamber of she who conceived me.

Having found her king again, she is more determined than ever not to lose him, and to seek once again that place of intimacy with him.

In fact, by bringing him to her home and the very place of her birth in this manner, she is showing as plainly as she possibly can that she wants to share her family and her whole life with him. Her heart is set on becoming his bride.

She is wise in this.

What happens far too often is that, when we become conscious that we have lost our fellowship with God, we start seeking Him again. But then, when his favour is restored and

He begins once more to pour out his blessings upon us, we get so excited about these initial experiences that we become preoccupied with trying to perpetuate them, and fail to press through to receive all that He has for us.

That has been the sad lesson of many a revival that has failed to achieve its full potential. The initial life-giving rush of God's spirit into dry and barren hearts is often spectacular, like a flash flood after a drought, and the experience is exhilarating. But the true fruits of God's favour are not found in such events any more than the land itself is made fertile by that first rush of water.

It is only as the flood waters are allowed to soak into the thirsty fields, often through a laborious process of irrigation, that the land bears its full fruit. And it is only if we are prepared to make a deep and lasting commitment of our lives to Him, to follow through on his purpose for our lives – forsaking all else – that we will ultimately achieve the true fruitfulness that He intends for us.

That exhortation again! (3:5)

5I have charged you, O daughters of Jerusalem, by the gazelles, and by the hinds of the field: do not awaken or stir up love until it desires.

Now notice again the charge concerning love.

What does it mean? This is not the time to discuss it yet: but let me give you a clue to ponder…

The first time she said these words was when she had just found herself so utterly overwhelmed by love that she was at the end of her strength. Now, she is saying it again, having just been through an experience where, drawn by her yearning, she has been obliged to go out into the 'beyond' for her king. And in both cases, she has just entered into a place of deep intimacy…

THE MARRIAGE OF THE KING (3:6-5:1)

The Coming of the King (3:6-10)

⁶*Who is this coming up from the wilderness like columns of smoke, perfumed with myrrh and frankincense, with all the merchant's powders?*

⁷*See his couch – Solomon's own; sixty mighty men about it, of the mighty men of Israel.* ⁸*They all grasp swords, trained in battle: each man with his sword at his thigh in case of fear in the night.*

⁹*King Solomon made himself a palanquin from the wood of Lebanon.* ¹⁰*He made its pillars of silver, its base of gold, its seat of purple, the midst of it paved with love – of the daughters of Jerusalem.*

A place of privilege

Now Solomon comes to claim his bride. Making the point that he is Lord of the far domains, he comes from the wilderness to the city in a magnificent palanquin – like a mobile stateroom, normally carried by slaves, servants or animals. (Wheeled carriages had poor suspension in those days!)

> Did the king ride on the backs of enemy slaves or of his own servants? We don't know: but just think how different this selfsame task would have been for them. For an enemy it would be the ultimate humiliation to have this king ride upon your back: but, for one who loved him, it would have been an honour and privilege to bear his king on his shoulders!
>
> *The real character of a task is not defined by the task itself: but by the motive of the one doing it.*

Inside was a couch where the king and his bride could recline in comfort. The one fortunate enough to be his bride is destined to share these benefits – and more beside.

His approach is visible a long way off, like a rising pillar of smoke. Normally, for a caravan arriving in this fashion, the cloud would be dust, and the weary travellers would arrive, very hot and smelly from their travels: but not the king: wherever he goes, there is fragrance.

But his presence is not just the place of sweet fragrance and shelter from the heat of the sun: it is also a place of safety, surrounded by the king's guard. It is a place of splendour, comfort and love.

But if the presence of an earthly king is a place of fragrance and splendour, what of the presence of God himself? As He promised Moses, *"My Presence will go with you, and I will give you rest"*. (Ex. 33:14.)

Even if our external circumstances are like a desert, with wild beasts or men trying to destroy us: there is still an inner place we can enter, close into his presence. It is a place of supreme rest and sweetness, where we can sit, lie or stand in awe of the majesty of God. And it is a place of safety from any attempt to harm our spirit.

'Peace I leave with you,' said, Jesus. 'My peace I give

> *He who dwells in the secret place of the Most High will rest in the shadow of the Almighty. I will say of Yahweh, "He is my refuge and my fortress; my God, in whom I trust."*
> *For he will deliver you from the snare of the fowler, and from the deadly pestilence. He will cover you with his feathers. Under his wings you will take refuge. His faithfulness is your shield and rampart. You shall not be afraid of the terror by night, nor of the arrow that flies by day; nor of the pestilence that walks in darkness, nor of the destruction that wastes at noonday. A thousand may fall at your side, and ten thousand at your right hand; but it will not come near you. You will only look with your eyes, and see the recompense of the wicked.*
> *Because you have made Yahweh your refuge, and the Most High your dwelling place, no evil shall happen to you, neither shall any plague come near your dwelling.* (Psalm 91:1-10.)

to you; not as the world gives, give I to you. Don't let your heart be troubled, neither let it be fearful.' (John 14:27.)

And Paul, mindful of this, tells us, *"In nothing be anxious, but in everything, by prayer and petition with thanksgiving, let your requests be made known to God. And the peace of God, which surpasses all understanding, will guard your hearts and your thoughts in Christ Jesus"*. (Phil. 4:6-7.)

But this is not a place into which just anyone may come. It is not enough to merely be an admirer, or one of the crowd of onlookers. Just as, in the song, it is reserved for the king and his bride so, too, this position of peace and security belongs only to those who have yielded their lives to Christ.

A place of authority

This was also a position of royal authority, from which Solomon and his queen would gaze down upon their subjects, and even upon their enemies. And Paul reminds us concerning Jesus that, *'He put all things in subjection under his feet, and gave him to be head over all things,'* (Eph 1:22) and then that God *'raised us up with him, and made us to sit with him in the heavenly places in Christ Jesus.'* (Eph 2:6.)

This means that all things are also under our feet, including all our enemies, seen and unseen. We have authority over them – but only to the extent that we live in our King's favour and speak and act according to his will. Too many Christians glibly quote these verses from Ephesians, then start trying to command this or that and wonder why they come to grief.

It was exactly the same for the new queen. Becoming queen did not confer on her any legal powers of her own. But because she had the king's ear – and his devotion – few would dare defy her. So her first priority must be to maintain her place of intimacy with Him. But the king will not permit her to rule Him: so she must learn to understand his desires and ask and command accordingly. Then, and only then, will she have true authority. For a superb example of this process in action, see Esther 4:11-8:8.

In the same way, Jesus tells us, *'If you remain in me, and my words remain in you, you will ask whatever you desire, and it will be done for you.'* (Jn 15:7.)

As we shall see, Solomon and his companions did not always travel in such luxury. And our relationship with Christ will not only consist of such comfortable 'throne room' experiences.

When it comes to facing the wilderness of 'the real world,' there will be times when the cosy surroundings of the palanquin seem a million miles away, and we are forced to face life in the raw.

At such times it is important to remember that sitting in the palanquin was not the cause of the new queen's favour, but the result of it. As long as she stays close to him, his favour, authority and protection will cover her, no matter what the situation. At no time does the king ever require his bride to face the wilderness alone. In the same way, regardless of external circumstances, we always have that right of access, that authority and that security of living in our King's favour and under his protection. Always, this principle remains true: that no matter what dangers and difficulties we may face, the place of safety is in his presence. And He will never leave us or forsake us, for He has promised, "*I am with you always, even to the end of the age.*" (Matt. 28:20.)

The unfulfilled vision (3:10b)

Some versions, such as the AV, render the end of verse 10 as 'paved with love, *for* the daughters of Jerusalem;' though the general consensus of scholars seems to be that '*by* the daughters of Jerusalem' is more accurate. But, having said that, there seems little doubt that there was a great deal of reciprocal affection between Solomon and the 'Daughters.' They loved him, and he loved them.

It is clear from this song that Solomon understood very well how the love of the king could be the ultimate dream for a young maiden like this. And it also shows us how much personal delight he found in giving and receiving such love.

But here, too, was the root of his greatest folly.

Solomon glimpsed an ideal of a king who could satisfy the deepest longings of all his subjects – a king who would love every single one of them, and by doing so bring meaning, joy and purpose to their lives.

In this song, Solomon, carried away with love for one who has set her heart on knowing him, expounds his vision of what such love can accomplish in her life. He dreamt of the fulfilment of this vision. But he tried to fulfil that role himself – and that was something no mere man could ever do.

It is difficult enough for a man to love one woman adequately, giving her all the time and affection she needs and is entitled to expect. Even this seemingly simple and pleasurable task can make such demands on us that it is a real struggle at times to balance it with God's call to give Him first place in our lives. Add another wife, and that halves the reserves of love that we have to give – or else it begins to squeeze God out of his rightful place.

> *Now king Solomon loved many foreign women, together with the daughter of Pharaoh, women of the Moabites, Ammonites, Edomites, Sidonians, and Hittites; of the nations concerning which Yahweh said to the children of Israel, "You shall not go among them, neither shall they come among you; for surely they will turn away your heart after their gods". Solomon joined to these in love. He had seven hundred wives, princesses, and three hundred concubines; and his wives turned away his heart. For it happened, when Solomon was old, that his wives turned away his heart after other gods; and his heart was not perfect with Yahweh his God, as was the heart of David his father.*
>
> (1 Kings 11: 1-4)

In fact, years before, Moses specifically warned that a king must not '*multiply wives to himself, that his heart not turn away.*' (Deut 17:17.) But Solomon, in his misdirected pursuit of this vision of perfect kingly love, ignored this warning; and his many wives and concubines became his undoing.

But what Solomon glimpsed and foolishly tried to grasp, is exactly what *is* fulfilled in Jesus. He, being God, can indeed love each one who comes to Him in such a way that it is as if there is only He and that one. So in Jesus all the potential of this vision is realised: and what was, in Solomon, a wedding-day dream he could never bring to completion becomes a wonderful reality that completely, continuously and unfailingly satisfies the hearts of all who put their trust in Him.

The King claims his Bride (3:11)

[11]*Go out, daughters of Zion, and see king Solomon with the crown with which his mother crowned him on his wedding day – the day of his heart's rejoicing!*

And so, we come to the marriage, and the king has claimed the Seeker as his bride.

This is the turning point in our story. Up till now, our Seeker is only that, despite being so deeply loved by the king. But from this moment, she is his bride and queen. All the privileges we have just been speaking about are now truly hers. For as she yields herself to him, so he gives himself to her.

To illustrate just what this means, allow me to exercise a little fancy for a moment. Suppose our Seeker's brothers had been angry with her over debts that she had incurred and was unable to pay. Right up to this moment she carried the responsibility for those debts. According to the law of the land the creditor was entitled to demand her as his slave in payment of her debt: and only one person – her nearest kinsman – had the legal power to force a creditor to accept payment in return for her release. Even the king could not interfere, because his duty was to uphold the law.

But from the moment that she surrenders her life to the king, she and her husband are united; and he becomes her nearest kinsman. No debt she could possibly owe comes anywhere near the price that Solomon is capable of paying: so the debt will be cancelled and the creditor cannot touch her.

Why do I emphasise this point, when we actually have no idea what the problem was with her brothers? It is because we need to understand that it is not sufficient to simply know *about* the love of Jesus, and the price He paid for our sins on the Cross. There has to be a voluntary handover of your life and uniting with Him before He can rightfully take responsibility for your guilt and free you from your past. You must make this decision for yourself. No-one else can do it for you. If you have not yet taken this step, please, please, do so now.

Jesus said, '*whoever commits sin is a slave of sin.*' (John 8:34.) Until you yield to Him as your Saviour and Lord, you are not his. You remain a slave to sin. It is your debt and even God cannot take it from you. But when you become his, all He has is yours; and you are free.

For the king, to have his bride is better than all his riches. This is 'the day of the gladness of his heart.' As Solomon's original request to God for wisdom showed, his people were his wealth; and he loved them more than all his possessions. How great then, must be his delight at this one, so beautiful in his estimation, and so utterly committed to him?

But, precious as she was to him, Solomon did not have to buy the life of his bride with his own blood, as Jesus did for us. How much greater then, is Jesus' delight when we give ourselves unreservedly back to Him?

Some may say, 'But, surely, we do not actually become the Bride of Christ until He returns; so how can this apply to us, now?'

I could answer that, although the marriage of the Lamb to his Bride, the New Jerusalem (Rev 21), is not depicted as taking place until the coming of the new heaven and earth, we are nevertheless already married to Him individually by virtue of the New Birth, as explained in Romans 7:1-6. I could also point out that, when Paul says, 'we are saved by hope,' in Romans 8:24, he uses a special tense that carries the meaning, 'we are saved, we are being saved and we shall be saved.' So, although the final fulfilment awaits us in heaven, we are beginning to experience the benefits even now.

But I think it is more sensible to simply acknowledge that few, if any, physical examples can perfectly illustrate all aspects of a spiritual truth. Solomon himself is a flawed example; and even a perfect human marriage could not fully illustrate the depths of intimacy, surrender and fulfilment to be found in our relationship with God.

It seems to me that a Christian's relationship with Christ is more akin to an unending cycle of revelation, deeper commitment and closer intimacy, rather like getting married over and over again, with an ever-increasing intensity of love. Nor do I think this process will end even when we finally stand as citizens of that new City, his beloved people, the New Jerusalem.

Why do I believe this? We are told that there are three things that will always endure: faith, hope and love (see 1 Cor 13:13). Notice that it is not love alone – or even just faith and love – that lasts forever; but also hope. But Romans 8:24 says, *'hope that is seen is not hope.'* So this tells me that, for all eternity, there must always be some new, unseen horizons, new discoveries, new experiences to stretch and increase our faith and lead us into an ever-deeper awe of, and intimacy with, our wonderful God and Lover.

The Beauty of the Bride (4:1-5)

[1]How fair you are, my darling. How fair you are! Your eyes are like doves' behind your veil; your hair like a flock of goats coming down from mount Gilead. [2]Your teeth are like a flock of sheep that have been shorn, that have come up from the wash; every one bearing twins, and none of them bereaved. [3]Your lips are like a thread of scarlet, and your speech lovely. Your temples are like a piece of pomegranate behind your veil. [4]Your neck is like the tower of David, built as an armoury, on which hang a thousand bucklers – all shields of mighty men. [5]Your two breasts are like two gazelle fawns – twins – grazing among the lilies.

Even while the bride is still veiled, the king praises her beauty. The imagery is lavish. He is thrilled with her.

Do we really understand just how much delight Jesus takes in us? 'But,' we say, 'I'm no beautiful princess!' Neither was she, when the king first found her, sun-scorched, despised and shy. She is splendid now because he saw her potential and made her so.

And in just the same way Jesus takes us, all messed-up as we are, and as we fall ever deeper in love with Him, yielding ourselves to his care and moulding, He makes us

'Well,' you may still think, 'she was intrinsically beautiful: I'm not!' But she was messed-up on the inside too. Our bodies are just a temporary covering. God looks much deeper than that. He made you in His image; and, no matter how badly marred that may be at the moment, He is able and willing to restore you.

beautiful; singing over us with delight as, step by step, first one aspect, then another, is transformed by his power.

Will You Share my Heart? (4:6-11)

The scent of the Beyond (4:6-7)

⁶*Until the day dawns, and the shadows flee, I will go away to the mountain of myrrh, and to the hill of frankincense.*
⁷*You are all fair, my darling; with not a blemish in you.*

The king's next comment may seem strange to us. What is he doing, apparently going away, at a time like this? But this was a very different culture from our own; and the king did not normally spend the night with his queen.

We have already said, and will see again as we read on, that Solomon was a shepherd king; a man with a heart for the wild and unreached places, and for his people, wherever they were. He could never rest long in his palace when he had his people and kingdom to watch over.

> In those days the queen normally lived and slept in the royal harem, where she was waited on by women and eunuchs. She would be summoned to the king, or he would visit her, to enjoy their times of intimacy together. But, apart from eunuchs and children, no other man was ever admitted.

But this time, he has something else on his mind as well. Not only does he want to go and view his realm: but He also longs to bless the bride he loves. How can he do this, unless he can help her understand the wonder of the wild places?

Even men who hate shopping may sometimes be caught browsing the perfumery departments of the big department stores. For we all know how much delight the fairer sex can find in a few drops of liquid that, somehow, seems to cost its weight in gold! But in Solomon's day, the finest fragrances were not necessarily found in the market place: rather, they could be harvested fresh from the hills. And so, with a final reassuring statement of his total delight in her, he sets off to bring back and show her something of the beauty of those far-off places – the fragrance of wild myrrh and incense.

My heart is yours (4:8-11)

*[8]Enter in with me from Lebanon, my bride, with me from Lebanon:
look around from the top of Amana, from the top of Shenir and
Hermon, from the lions' lairs, from the mountain ranges of the
leopards.*
*[9]You have enlightened my heart, my sister, my bride; you have
enlightened my heart with one of your eyes, with one pendant of
your neck. [10]How beautiful have been your lovings, my sister, my
bride! How much better have your lovings been than wine, and the
fragrance of your oils than all spices! [11]Your lips, my bride, drip
like a honeycomb: honey and milk are under your tongue; and the
fragrance of your garments is like the fragrance of Lebanon.*

Verse 8 begins a new section. It seems to me that he is
probably returning from his trip, inspired once more both with
the beauties and challenges of the mountains – and with his love
for her. He pleads for her to come and let him share it all with
her.

(My guess, however, is that she is less thrilled than he is at
the mention of lions and leopards!)

But, whatever her reaction to that suggestion just now, he is
utterly in love with her. His heart is hers, many times over. And
for him the spices he bears, precious as they are, and the places
he has been, wonderful though they were, are nowhere near as
precious as her love.

We, too, have a Shepherd King, whose heart is constantly
yearning for the as-yet unconquered and unreached places and
peoples of his domain and the hidden wonders of his creation.
And He wants to share it all with us. If we choose to go with
Him, some of it will be strange and beautiful, and some will be
wild and dangerous.

Many prefer to stay in their comfort zones, enjoying the
occasional scent of distant adventure. We love to read
missionary tales of miraculous deliverances and answered
prayer. We even acknowledge how such testimonies have
encouraged and increased our faith. But if we never take the

risk of letting the King lead *us* there – into situations that might expose us to difficulty, discomfort or danger – our so-called faith never becomes more than ineffectual daydreams, like a sickly plant that has never seen the full light of day.

If we will not go with Him, we will never see the world as He sees it, never begin to feel for it the way He feels for it, and never truly share his heart.

He loves us so much. He only wants the best for us. His heart is ours, and our love is far more important to Him than any service we can render. Will we let Him have our hearts, and learn to share his vision and his yearnings?

The Secret Garden (4:12-5:1)

Will you open up to me? (4:12-15)

[12]*A locked-up garden is my sister, my bride; a locked-up (store) heap*[1], *a sealed fountain.*
[13]*Your shoots are a paradise of pomegranates, with choice fruits; henna with spikenard;* [14]*spikenard and saffron; calamus and cinnamon; with all (kinds of) trees of frankincense, myrrh and aloes; (and) with all the chief spices.*
[15]*A fountain of the gardens, a well of living waters, flowing from Lebanon.*

The king can see that, inwardly, she has so much to offer: but she has been keeping others out of her life, like a secret walled garden.

Knowing what we do of her former life, it is easy to understand why she should be this way. Partly, it would be out of fear of being hurt again, as she had been in the past. But also, as is implied later in the Song, it was because she had previously been unwilling to commit herself fully to any man, having never found anyone she felt was worthy of her absolute trust.

---

[1] Many translations say 'spring:' but 'heap' is the primary meaning. It is used to describe a wave of the sea: but is not translated as 'spring' anywhere else in scripture.

Now, she needs to fully open herself up to her husband and king. But, even though she is now his, he will not simply take possession. Rather, he waits to be invited, and gently coaxes her by painting a beautifully evocative picture of the amazing potential of her love to satisfy his soul.

Again, in our own relationship with Jesus, we see the same patient coaxing. Often, we wonder why it is that, once we have invited Him into our lives, things don't just suddenly change. But He does not want to demand more of us than we are truly willing to give.

> Sometimes, like Peter on the night of Jesus' betrayal, we delude ourselves that we are more ready than we really are; and we complain that we made ourselves available and were ignored. Be thankful for it! When He sees that you are truly ready, He will take you at your word.

As our Lord, He could command us to do whatever He wants: but as our lover, He patiently encourages us and waits until we are truly ready.

He wants our love; and true love is always given voluntarily.

Help me! (4:16)

[16] *Awake, O north wind; and come, O south! Make my garden breathe, that its spices may flow out! Let my beloved come into his garden, and eat its choice fruits.*

Won over by his love, and finally realising that she can truly be all that he declares her to be, she resolves to let down her defences and yield herself to him. But, having spent years in inward isolation, shutting off her feelings for fear of being hurt or exploited, she finds that she cannot now release them as easily as she would like to. So, on the one hand, she calls on the wind to help her and, on the other, she begs the king not to wait any longer.

Many of us, before we come to Jesus, have so thoroughly walled ourselves in against hurt and fear of exploitation that we are no longer capable of freely expressing our natural human emotional responses. So we need help to open ourselves up to God.

In the spiritual realm, wind is almost always symbolic of the Holy Spirit; one of whose chief functions is to help us become the people we are meant to be. We may not be capable of much of a response ourselves; but we don't have to be. If we will only invite the Holy Spirit to work upon our lives, He will. He will rekindle our emotions and remould our character, to make us, in the words of St Paul, 'a sweet aroma of Christ.' (2Cor 2:15.)

I myself was in this position. As a teenager I had suppressed my emotions so completely that, even if you had told me my entire family had died in a car crash, I would not have batted an eyelid. So, when I became a Christian, my main problem was how to obey Jesus' first commandment: 'Love the Lord your God with all your heart, and with all your soul and with all your mind and with all your strength' (Mt. 12:30). I said to Him, 'Lord, how can I love You? I don't even know what love feels like. Help me!'

And He showed me that I didn't have to struggle to drum up 'lovey-dovey' feelings or anything like that. All He asked of me was that I allow Him to work in my life, and that I love Him in the one way I was capable of – by simply doing things that I felt would please Him.

For me, the releasing of my emotions has been a very gradual process – and, indeed is still ongoing: but the change has been so radical that nowadays, when I speak of it, I often feel the contrast so sharply that I wonder if I am going to be believed.

And Jesus Himself will come into our lives if we really want Him to. In spite of all the junk and baggage that is there, He will accept us just as we are until, eventually, we learn to become all that He wants us to be.

Intimacy requires privacy (5:1a)

[1]I have come into my garden, my sister, my bride. I have gathered my
   myrrh with my spice; I have eaten my honeycomb with my honey;
   I have drunk my wine with my milk.

In a manner reminiscent of the old movies – when, as two lovers engaged in a passionate embrace, the picture would discreetly fade away to the next scene – what happens next is left to our imagination. Instead, the song picks up the story in the sweet aftermath of their time together, as the king tells her how delightful it has been for him.

This is quite unlike the modern desire to be as explicit as possible. But it is more than just a comment on artistic style: Solomon is the one who is actually writing the song; so what he does here as an author reflects his own attitude to her womanhood and personal needs. He recognises that intimacy requires privacy. If she is to be fully open to him, she needs to be alone with him, and to know that what passes between them is for him and her alone.

When Jesus spoke about prayer, He said, *'enter into your inner room, and having shut your door, pray to your Father who is in secret, and your Father who sees in secret will reward you openly.'* (Mt. 6:6.) There is a depth of intimacy in prayer that cannot be realised in a public meeting, no matter how great and awesome the sense of God's presence may be. So, if you want to deepen your relationship with Him, take time to be alone together.

The King always comes with his friends (5:1b)

[1(b)] *… Eat friends! Drink! Yes, drink abundantly, beloved ones!*

The last part of this verse is vital if we are to understand the events that follow. Immediately after this wonderful, intimate time that they have just enjoyed together, the king calls his friends for a party!

Do you think this is what his new bride wanted? Absolutely not! She was more probably making plans for a candlelit meal and a quiet evening together, with minstrels playing discreetly in the garden, or something equally soothing and romantic.

Instead she is suddenly plunged into a flurry of activity, with unfamiliar faces and unexpected demands being made of her. For one so fresh from her previous background, this must have been a terrible ordeal, and she probably longed to just run away and hide until it was all over. (Maybe she did!)

To her, his actions may well have seemed really insensitive: but, much as he loves her, he is not her king only; he is the shepherd king of Israel. He cannot ignore the needs of his other friends and subjects for very long; so if she is going to stay close to her king, she will have to learn to accept this invasion by his friends.

Many of us have had similar experiences. Jesus has picked us up, sorted us out, and, never forcing Himself on us, encouraged us to open up to Him. If only our relationship had stayed on that cosy one-to-one basis, everything would have been wonderful.

But then has come the point where He started exposing us to the needs and demands of others. Because He loves unselfishly, those who profess love for Him must learn to do the same (1 Jn 4:20-1). What's more, being the kind of person He is, the people He chooses to befriend are not the kind we would choose for ourselves. Yet it is precisely such unconditional and accepting love, when directed towards us, that thrills our hearts and makes us feel so secure. So we cannot ask Him to exclude others without denying the very love we ourselves crave.

> *Those who welcome the King into their lives must learn to welcome his friends as well.*

The trouble is that there are so many of them, with so many needs! Sooner or later, many of us have tried to close the door on their demands, telling ourselves that it is one thing for Jesus to enter our private space: but all these others are just too much!

A CRISIS OF TRUST (5:2-6:3)

When the King Comes Knocking (5:2)

²In sleep, my heart awakes… The voice of my beloved knocking!
Open to me, my sister, my darling, my dove, my perfect one; for
my head is filled with dew, and my locks with the drops of the
night

Later in the night, the king comes again, asking her to let him in.

Why, do you suppose? He doesn't seem to be enthusing about the wonderful places he has just been, and he isn't suggesting any new adventure. In fact, the only things he is saying is that she is precious to him and that he himself is wet with dew.

You see, although it can get very hot during the day in Palestine, the nights can be very cold, causing a heavy dew. But, even so, people aren't likely get their hair filled with dew unless they have been out in the cold for a very long time and are themselves pretty thoroughly chilled.

It looks as if, once more, the shepherd king has been out and about, watching over his realm. Such care has taken its toll on him; and now he is returning, cold and wet, longing for the warmth and comfort of her embrace.

But now I want you to pause for a moment, and consider our very own Shepherd King, Jesus. Picture Him as He travels the streets of your town looking, in first one home then another, at the state of his beloved creation. Does He find much there to warm his heart?

In this house, they are having a row; in this one, they are watching an X-rated video. Here, his name is only mentioned as an expression of disgust. There, a beloved daughter is dying, but all the forlorn hope of the parents is pinned on the doctors and their only thought of God is, 'If God is good, how can all this be happening to us?'

I think Jesus' heart must break over scenes such as this. Was Calvary really worth it, when people continue to live in such misery? I know He sees the end from the beginning: but that does not make Him immune from the present pain.

Just as He agonised in Gethsemane at the pain that awaited Him, so I am sure He feels the impact of our present sufferings and is sickened by it. Indeed, we are expressly told that in Jesus, we have one who fully understands, having suffered it Himself (see Heb 4:15). 'Cold and wet' strikes me as a pretty good description of the way it must make Him feel.

Now, how do you suppose He feels as He comes to your door? What do you think He is longing for?

I believe that He is looking for an answer to the question, 'Was it worth it?' *You are that answer*. He longs for the warmth of your spiritual embrace – for a response of love from you that says, 'Stay with me a while. You mean all the world to me.' But how will you actually respond?

You're probably saying to yourself, 'Yes, but He doesn't actually come knocking at my door like that.' Is that so? Well, what of those times when you have your feet up, perhaps watching the TV, reading or just trying to decide how you'd like to spend the next half-hour. Then the thought comes to you; when was the last time you just spent some extra time with God, either praying or reading his word? You may even be quite busy, when suddenly the urge comes to make some time for Him. Jesus is at your door: will you welcome Him in from the cold of the world?

Do you have any idea how much of a blessing, relief and comfort it is to Jesus, personally, when you do?

The Things that Hold us Back (5:3-5)

Present comfort, past memory, future fear (5:3)

³I have stripped off my tunic; should I be putting it on? I have washed my feet; should I be soiling them?

At first glance, her reasons for not opening at once seem so trivial – she has taken off her normal day-garment, and washed her feet. But this is her husband! Can she really be worried about him seeing her in her night-dress? Or about getting her feet dirty on the bedroom floor? Can she really love him so little, or love her own comfort so much?

If these were her only reasons, then she is suffering a serious lack of love: though it has to be admitted that, even as lovers, we can at times be incredibly selfish in our attitudes to those we should love the most. Likewise, we as Christians have to hang our heads in shame at the number of times we have let our own comfort and interests win out over love for our Lord, and have chosen TV and suchlike trivia before availability to God.

But there is, I believe, a deeper, and much more serious reason for her reaction.

Remember how their last time together had ended? After a time of intense one-to-one intimacy, he had shocked her by calling for a party with his other friends. Suddenly, she was confronted by a whole host of demands that she hadn't bargained for. She is still feeling emotionally bruised by that experience, and afraid of what he might ask of her next.

I suggested above that, almost certainly, what the king wanted was to come in and enjoy the warmth of her embrace: but that is not how she is thinking. A wife doesn't need to put on her day clothes for that. She is probably thinking, 'Who does he want me to meet now?' She shouldn't get her feet seriously dirty just by going to open the door. These were royal apartments – surely they had servants to keep the floors clean! But is he about to come up with another idea for a nocturnal excursion?

Her problem now is one of mistrust. Because she is still holding onto an unresolved memory of her previous experience with the party (perhaps even without consciously realising it), she doubts his motives and misbelieves the things he says to her.

Jesus did not choose the easy way for Himself and, much as He loves you, He will not always choose it for you either. He was despised, rejected, emotionally – and even physically – bruised; and at times we will be too. How we respond to those experiences is of critical importance; because all too easily a past memory can become the root of a future fear, as has happened here. All our fears for the future have their roots in uncertainties over the reality and strength of Jesus' love for us; for perfect love casts out fear (1 Jn 4:18).

When the disciples were beaten by the Sanhedrin for their testimony about Jesus, they went away 'rejoicing because they had been counted worthy of suffering disgrace for the Name.' They saw their suffering as a positive affirmation of Jesus' confidence in, and identification with, themselves. As a result, 'daily in the temple, and in every house, they ceased not to teach and preach Jesus Christ.' (Acts 5:41-2.) But when we allow ourselves to question his reasons for permitting our difficulties, we begin to doubt his love; so our relationship with Him, and the faith that flows from it, is undermined.

Future agenda can hinder present response (5:4-5)

⁴*My beloved stretched out his hand through the hole; and my innards cried out for him.* ⁵*I got up to open to my beloved; and my hands dripped with myrrh, my fingers with liquid myrrh on the handles of the lock.*

Our Seeker had not ceased to love her king: far from it. When she saw him trying to open the latch from outside, she could hold back no longer: but now she finds herself fumbling at the lock, for her hands are covered with myrrh. The AV describes this as 'sweet-smelling' myrrh: but the root meaning of the adjective is 'flowing.'

In its raw form, myrrh is a gum-like resin from the bark of a tree: but the active ingredients could be extracted by heating in olive oil to form oil of myrrh: which appears to be what is being described here. It was used as a purifying skin ointment and beauty treatment. For example, before Esther was brought to king Ahasuerus, she underwent 6 months of purification with oil of myrrh (Es 2:12). This would have been to ensure that, when finally presented to the king, her skin and complexion was as soft and flawless as possible.

I dare say our Seeker had a similar motive for using myrrh on her hands. She was planning for her next meeting with the king, and evoking the memory of his lovely description of her as a walled garden, flowing with the scent of precious perfumes. But, had she wiped her hands on the bedclothes and jumped up the moment she heard his voice, precious seconds might have been saved.

Sometimes, even with the best of intentions, the plans we devise for serving and pleasing the Lord can be in conflict with his own. There is no blame attached to this: indeed, the Lord takes pleasure in the fact that we desire to do such things (see inset). But as soon as it becomes apparent that there is any conflict between our plans and his, we need to quickly abandon our own, or they will become a hindrance to us, as happens here.

> But Yahweh said to David my father, 'Whereas it was in your heart to build a house for my name, you did well that it was in your heart: nevertheless you shall not build the house; but your son who shall come forth out of your body, he shall build the house for my name.'
>
> (2 Chron 6:8-9)

Many a noble spiritual endeavour has foundered because people failed to discern the moment when their future plans got in the way of what God wanted to do there and then.

Very often, this takes the form of holding back from giving now for fear that, if we do, we will not be able to carry out what we had planned to do later. The sad irony is that in many cases, had we given when prompted, God would have provided additional resources when the time came for the other. Whereas when we hold back, not only is the present opportunity lost but, because we have failed to heed God's voice, so is the later one.

Many a well-meaning Christian, for example, has set aside funds with which to serve the Lord when they retire, only to be overtaken by ill-health or other circumstances that have robbed them of the opportunity. Before you invest in such a future agenda, you need to be sure that God is not saying there is something else He wants you to do now. And if He subsequently tells you to blow it all, and lay on his altar the hard-won 'Isaac' of your future prospects; then trust Him and do it. He will provide whatever resources are needed to set the seal of his approval on your sacrifice.

The Perils of Mistrust (5:6-8)

⁶I opened to my beloved: but my beloved had turned away and passed on. My soul had gone out when he spoke. I sought him, but could not find him; I called him, but he did not answer.

⁷The watchmen going around the city found me. They struck me. They wounded me. The keepers of the walls lifted up my covering from me.

⁸I have charged you, O daughters of Jerusalem, if you find my beloved (this is) what you should tell him: that I am weak with love!

From Bad to Worse (5:6-8)

Our Seeker gets the door open: but she has allowed her doubts and hindrances to delay her for too long: he has gone again. But this time she does not hang about on her bed. She quickly sets out to search for him, calling out his name. However, there is no answer; and this time things do not turn out so well for her.

Firstly, she gets some rough treatment from the watchmen.

'Why is this?' you may wonder. Well, the watchmen were there to look out for any suspicious goings on. When she met them previously, she was still just a simple, unmarried girl, looking for her lover after some kind of upset between them. So what's unusual about that?

Her earlier comment, 'why should I be as one that veils herself' (see 1:7), suggests that previously she had not normally worn a veil. But now, as the king's wife, she did. What is more, no wife of the king had any business being out and about on her own in the city at night – she should be safe at home in the king's harem. Consequently, the watchmen would almost certainly have decided she was up to no good – perhaps a spy, or someone cheating on her husband. So they tore away her veil (a deep humiliation for someone in her position) to see who she really was. No doubt they got a severe shock when they did!

But, secondly, this time she does not find him; and eventually, desperate and faint with longing, she begs the other maidens to pass on a message if they see him.

So why is it that the consequences of her delay are more severe this time? After all, she had actually tried to open the door for him on this occasion (she hadn't before) and went out looking for him straight away. Is it because he is mad at her and has gone off in a huff? Apparently not, as we shall see later.

Her first problem is that she doesn't know where he has gone. The last time this happened, he had been calling her to accompany him out of the city; and that was where she found him. But this time he had been trying to come in to her; and she had left him outside. So she doesn't know where he was going and her mistrust has put her out of tune with him; so that she is misreading his actions and responses.

Her next problem is that she has wandered outside of his protection into an area where the king's bride had no business to be. Her motive was admirable: but her actions were desperate and ill advised. She is doing what we so often do when things go wrong: trying to remember what worked last time and repeating it, as if sorting out wounded relationships were a matter of a simple, 'Do this; do that,' formula.

Would she have found him more quickly, then, if she had simply stayed in her room and waited for him to return? Probably not, though she could have avoided the encounter with the watchmen. This is because her third problem, and the root of all the rest, lay within her: *nothing short of a change of heart attitude can ever fix the problem of mistrust.*

It only takes a tiny seed of mistrust to create havoc in our relationship with God. Satan knew this when he told Eve that God wouldn't let them eat from the tree of knowledge because then they would become like gods.

When unpleasant things happen to us whilst we are serving the Lord – as they surely will – it is essential that we do not allow this to disturb our confidence in Him, even if we do not understand why they happened. As long as we continue to trust, Satan is the loser (see Job 1:20-2:3): but, once we start to doubt Him, we begin digging a hole for ourselves from which there is no escape until we turn again from our mistrust and place our confidence in Him once more (Job 42:1-6).

Mistrust blinds us to his will, and causes us to move out of his protective covering. And, as long as it grips our hearts, even our attempts to rationalise our situation, or to figure out what He would have us do, only give the enemy additional opportunities to make things worse for us.

A word about the watchmen (5:7)

Before we leave these verses, it is worth asking, 'What about the watchmen?'

I don't suppose Solomon would have been too pleased when he learned how they had treated his bride. They were supposed to be protecting the king's people and possessions: instead, they had harmed her.

The sad truth is that, when we go astray in this manner, it is often God's own people who lay into us the most severely and hurt us most. They see us messing things up; but fail to understand what is really going on in our hearts. They do not see that, despite our stupid behaviour, we do really want to get things sorted out: so, instead of coming alongside to help, they condemn us and leave us more wounded than before.

But don't let us be too quick to condemn the watchmen either. If we would only be scrupulously honest here, we would probably have to admit that we have done the same to others ourselves. May God give us the grace to look beyond a person's outward behaviour to understand the cries of their heart.

The Excellence of the King (5:9-16)

⁹How is your beloved better than another beloved, O fairest among women? How is your beloved better than another beloved, that you charge us so?
¹⁰My beloved is radiant and ruddy (as Adam), (like) a standard-bearer amongst ten thousand. ¹¹His head is refined pure gold; his locks – bushy and black as a raven; ¹²his eyes like those of doves by rivers of waters, washed with milk, sitting in fullness; ¹³his cheeks – a bed of spices, (and) perfumed towers¹; his lips – lilies, dripping liquid myrrh; ¹⁴his hands – golden rolls² filled with gemstones: his belly – smooth ivory covered with sapphires; ¹⁵his legs – pillars of marble, fixed on bases of refined gold; his appearance like Lebanon, (as) outstanding as the cedars. ¹⁶His mouth is most sweet; he is altogether lovely! This is my beloved; and this – my friend, O daughters of Jerusalem.

No other can compare (5:9-16)

The daughters of Jerusalem respond to the Seeker's pleas with a challenge: what's so special about the one you love?

Now, you might have thought the answer was obvious: but these young women have not enjoyed the same intimacy with the king as our Seeker, though they have probably spent a fair bit of time running around after him and dreaming about the possibility. So, for them, the questions naturally arise, 'Is he really worth it?' 'Will he ever even notice me?' 'Perhaps I'd be better off settling for someone else.'

But for our Seeker, this challenge provides the impulse she needs to get her back on track, by forcing her to think again about just how wonderful her king really is.

---

¹ Every other biblical usage of this word indicates some kind of tower. But what does she mean? I suspect that she is referring to the appearance of his nostrils, seeming to rise up like towers beside his cheeks when she is lying cheek-to-cheek beside him. Otherwise, why is his nose missing from her description?

² Precise translation uncertain: but derived from a root meaning 'to roll.'

I will not attempt to expound on all the imagery she uses – it is easy enough to see she is saying that every aspect of him can only be compared to the most beautiful and excellent things that she can imagine. But there is one phrase that, if properly understood, sums up just how much better he is than any other; 'a standard-bearer amongst ten thousand.'

'Standard-bearer' is commonly translated as 'outstanding,' 'chief' or 'fairest.' At first sight, this is quite a compliment: but it doesn't rule out the possibility that, if you tried enough (twenty or fifty thousand, perhaps) you might find someone better.

But the full meaning is far stronger. The expression is a very unusual one and difficult to translate exactly. It is the passive participle of a verb meaning, 'to set up a banner.' (It is used again in 6:4 & 10; and the word 'banner' in 2:4 is derived from it.)

To illustrate this, imagine an army of ten thousand men, assembled in ranks ready for battle. To commemorate the occasion, you have been asked to take their photograph or paint a picture.

Now to even get a proper view of the entire army, you would have to stand so far back that individual faces would be unrecognisable – it would just be a sea of uniforms and vague faces. How, in all that crowd, could *any* one man stand out?

But, inexorably and unavoidably, you find that your eye *is* drawn to just one man: because over his head, waving proudly in the wind is a huge war-standard, marking the place where the king has taken up his position.

That is what this word means. She isn't just saying, 'He's the best of the bunch;' she is saying, 'Put him among a host of 10,000 men, and he will stand out as far above all the others as a war-standard over an army!' There is simply no competition.

While we are looking at this verse, the words 'radiant' (AV 'white') and 'ruddy' are interesting. 'Radiant' does not just mean 'white,' as it appears in many translations: but clear, dazzling and bright. It reminds me of those soap powder adverts. You know, here's a bunch of guys whose shirts have been washed in Brand X. They look quite clean until suddenly in walks the one whose shirt has just been washed in 'New Superwhite' – and he gleams so much that suddenly their shirts are grey in comparison! That's him – he outshines all the rest!

But 'ruddy,' on the other hand, is the ordinary Hebrew word for 'red:' so most translators have rendered it as 'ruddy,' interpreting it to mean 'a picture of health.' Doubtless he was; but there is another association that would have been familiar to her hearers. In Hebrew the stem of this word is identical to the name 'Adam' (so called because God formed him from the red dust of the earth). So to them she is not merely saying that he is 'red,' but also that he is 'like Adam' – an image of that perfect, first man.

The antidote to mistrust (5:16b)

She closes her description by declaring, '*This is my beloved; and this – my friend, O daughters of Jerusalem.*' The word 'beloved' is the one we discussed previously in 1:16, meaning not only a beloved one but also an uncle – the nearest kinsman. If she is declaring that he is lovely in every way – if he is such a beloved one, such an intimate friend – how can she mistrust him?

She can't! In making such a heartfelt declaration she has renewed her own confidence and trust in her king.

This is the antidote to mistrust: to look once more at the excellence of your King. How can one so wonderful ever be anything but utterly trustworthy, even if we have no idea why things should have turned out the way they did?

And, just as the Seeker was helped back into this place of trust by being challenged to declare why her lover was so special, so for us also, there is tremendous restorative power in speaking out the praises of our God. It is not that the mere recitation of any words can accomplish this: but as we speak out such things we are forced to consider whether or not we really believe them.

By the time the Seeker met the daughters of Jerusalem, she was already yearning to be back with her king. But, though this process may sometimes begin for us as a somewhat grudging and dutiful admission of his supremacy, as such words are affirmed as our convictions, and take root in our hearts, they are transformed into a declaration of true praise that breaks the chains of mistrust from our hearts and minds.

Restoration (6:1-3)

Passion is infectious (6:1)

¹Where has your beloved gone, O fairest among women? Where has your beloved turned aside? For we will seek him with you.

When looking at 1:4 we noted the implication that, if I am drawn, others will follow; and here we see this principle at work. The daughters of Jerusalem, who had just been asking, 'What's so special about your beloved?' are now galvanised into action, determined to find him for themselves.

Pastor, parent, teacher, carer, are you weary of trying to stir those you care for into love and devotion to the Lord? Stop trying; and just let yourself fall more deeply in love with Him – because passion is infectious. When they see you revitalised and thrilled afresh with the beauties of your Lord, those who have a true interest in Him will come asking how to find Him for themselves.

Back in harmony (6:2-3)

²My beloved has gone down to his garden; to the beds of spices, to graze (his flock) in the gardens and to gather lilies.
³I am my beloved's, and my beloved is mine: he grazes (his flock) among the lilies.

Up till now, the Seeker had no idea where her king had gone. But now, with her trust restored, she is back in tune with his thoughts and ways.

"Of course! He's not mad at me. He doesn't hold grudges. So where would he go? Where would a shepherd king go? Where would a shepherd king who is in love with me go? A king who said I was like a garden of spices (4:12-4)? A king who said my breasts were like twin fawns browsing among the lilies (4:5)?

"Of course! In the place he loves, grazing his flock, gathering lilies and waiting for me!"

Once our trust has been restored, it is always the same. We realise that He has never really been all that far away, patiently waiting to welcome us back into his arms. But we have to stop

> Some translations render 'to graze' as 'to feed.' But this is the same word as is used in 1:7-8, and it generally means to feed your flocks and herds, rather than yourself.
>
> The Hebrew 'garden' was not just a place to grow plants. Eden, for example, was a 'garden' where man and animals could both live and feed.

thrashing around trying to find Him, not really believing that He is there. *'For he who comes to God must believe that he exists, and that he is a rewarder of those who seek him.'* (Heb 11:6.)

Notice, however, that this restoration of trust is based on a fresh realisation of the character of her king; not on any sudden understanding of why he so abruptly interrupted their romantic evening.

We do not always understand why God acts as He does: although, over time as our relationship develops, we can often look back on such seasons with a fresh appreciation of his wisdom. But He is God and we are not: and sometimes the only answer He will give us is, *"Trust Me."*

THE GLORY OF THE BRIDE (6:4-7:9)

Irresistible in love (6:4-13)

You are awesome! (6:4-9)

⁴*You are as fair, my love, as Tirzah, as lovely as Jerusalem, as awesome as (a host of) banners!* ⁵*Turn away your eyes from me, for they have overcome me! Your hair is like a flock of goats coming down from mount Gilead.* ⁶*Your teeth are like a flock of sheep that have come up from the wash; every one bearing twins, and none of them bereaved.* ⁷*Liks a piece of pomegranate are your temples behind your veil...*
⁸*There are sixty queens, and eighty concubines – and virgins without number.* ⁹*(But) my dove, my perfect one, is (just) one; she is 'the' one of her mother, she is the pure one of her that bore her. The daughters saw her, and blessed her; the queens and concubines (also), and they praised her.*

The king now addresses his bride. He is bowled over by the splendour he sees in her. Tirzah was an ancient Canaanite royal city; and the Israelites were constantly singing of the beauties of Jerusalem. But she was not just beautiful; as he looks on this formerly insecure servant girl, he knows that now their love has given her an authority that even he cannot refuse. It is like being confronted with an entire army in all its proudest battle array, standards waving in the wind – a sight to make any one tremble!

When he sees that look of adoration in her eyes he is overcome with such a flood of emotions (the word used means 'to disturb, alarm, awe, confuse, make bold or proud'). He is helpless before her love, and thrilled by it – alarmed by the weakness he now feels in her presence, and at the same time bolder than ever because of it.

That is one of the contradictions of love – true love makes us simultaneously weak and strong. Weak because we know now just how much we need the other; and strong because together we are so much more than we ever were alone.

He begins to praise her again, repeating some of the beautiful descriptions he has used before. But then he breaks off – these just aren't adequate any more! She is simply the best he has ever known, above even queens of royal birth. He can find no fault in her. Even her peers and supposed superiors will have to acknowledge this.

At this point, we see another lovely thing. We recall how her youth was marred because she was despised by her brothers and sisters (1:6): but now she is openly proclaimed as her mother's favourite! Whether she was always her favourite, we do not know (maybe the way she looked towards her mother for assistance in her relationship (3:4 and 8:2) indicates that there always was a special bond there). But now those years of despising and rejection are rolled away as she stands in full and open acknowledgement of her worth.

Amazing as it may seem, this is how Jesus feels about us, as we fall deeper and deeper in love with Him. We so easily forget that He, who had all of heaven at his disposal, gave it all up, enduring shame and sorrow – for what purpose? Scripture says it was, *'for the joy that was set before Him.'* (Heb 12:2.) What joy? The Father's special gift to Him – you and I! (Jn 17:6.) And He endured the cross so that He could secure our salvation and make that love relationship with Himself possible.

You may find it hard to believe that you could ever be so valuable and wonderful to Him – that you could ever be so transformed by his love that you, too, will stand higher in his estimation than all the royalty of the earth. But that is his destiny for you (1 Pet 2:9). And the very fact that He was prepared to make such a sacrifice tells us plainly that He is utterly convinced of his ability to make it happen.

What happened to you? (6:10-13)

¹⁰*Who is she who looks out like the morning; fair as the moon, pure as the sun, and awesome as (a host of) banners?*

¹¹*I went down to the garden of nuts to see the fresh greenery of the valley, and to see if the vine had budded, and the pomegranates blossomed.* ¹²*Before I knew it, my soul had made me like the chariots of my noble people!*

¹³*Return, return, O Shulamite! Return, return, that we may behold you. What do you behold in the Shulamite? Like the dancing of two camps!*

What a transformation this is! Can this really be the same girl – this dazzling, awe-inspiring beauty? What has got into her?

In response, she relates how it had been before she met the king. Judging from 2:11-13, their meeting appears to have been in the early spring. She tells how she went down to the 'garden of nuts' looking for signs of early spring growth. Nuts were last year's crop (dry, in a tough shell; not sweet and succulent like grapes and pomegranates): but the new season's fruit was a long way off. It was a time of scarcity and longing for something new, for the return of hope.

And then, she met him! Suddenly, she was seized by love, and after him like a speeding chariot! There is debate as to whether the Hebrew 'Ammi-nadib' was a person noted for his fast chariots, or means 'my people, the Nadib,' or, 'my willing (or noble) people.' But whichever it is, the implication is clear enough: there was no stopping her now!

Opinions also differ as to the speakers in v. 13. I incline to the view that it is the daughters of Jerusalem calling her back, wanting to know more about her and the transformation that has taken place in her life.

The term, 'Shulamite,' used only here, is generally taken as a reference to her city of origin: but some lexicons translate it as 'the perfect' or 'the peaceful' – either of which provides a lovely picture of the transformation that has taken place in her life.

> This verse has led to speculation that the Seeker is David's half-wife, Abishag the Shunamite. This seems unlikely (see Introduction); but it is not impossible that she could have been a younger relative.

The meaning of the last part of the verse is also subject to some debate. The literal rendering is, 'Dance[1] of the Mahanaim.' 'Mahanaim' is both a biblical place name and a word meaning 'two camps (or, armies).' This may be a particular sort of dance: but it could also be an allusion to a custom that still persists among some nomadic peoples of North Africa.

When wandering tribes meet, providing they are friendly, they may hold a communal celebration dance. This is a particular opportunity for the young men and women to meet and attract partners. Naturally, each will strive to outdo the others and attract the most promising member of the opposite sex. Taken this way, it is probably saying that, single-handedly, her exuberance matches that of such a gathering, and that she is the star performer every young man would long for.

> But there's another interesting association here. The Biblical Mahanaim got its name because it is the place where Jacob and his family were met by a band of angels as he returned to the Promised Land. (See Gen 32:1-2.)
>
> Did the angels dance when they met him? Now that would have been some sight!

What happened to her? She fell in love with the king!

Without Jesus, the King of Kings, life is just existence; trying to cope through the hard and barren times; then looking for something better before the hard times come again. But, when we meet and fall in love with Him, He changes everything! We forget about the things we were looking for in our delight at

---

[1] The AV substitution of 'company' for 'dance' is speculative – every other biblical instance of this word clearly means 'dance' or 'dancing.'

finding Him. Then, on coming into our lives, He changes us so that, though we were once weak and lacked any real basis for believing in our worth, we grow to become strong in Him; his bride; children, kings and priests of the living God.

The King's Delight (7:1-9)

[1]How beautiful are your feet in sandals, noble daughter! The curves of your thighs are like wrought jewellery, the work of a master's hands. [2]Your navel is like a rounded offering-bowl, never lacking mingled wine: your belly like a heap of wheat surrounded by lilies. [3]Your two breasts are like two gazelle fawns – twins. [4]Your neck is like a tower of ivory; your eyes like the fish pools in Heshbon, by the gate of Bathrabbim: your nose like the tower of Lebanon looking toward Damascus. [5]Your head is like Carmel upon you, and the hair of your head like (a) purple (robe); the king is bound in its folds.
[6]How beautiful and how pleasant you have been, O love, in delights!
[7]This stature of yours resembles a palm tree; and your breasts, clusters of grapes. [8]I said, 'Let me climb the palm tree, let me take hold of its tips: and let your breasts be like clusters of the vine, the smell of your nose like apricots [9]and your palate like best wine.'
It flows down smoothly for my beloved, gently moving the sleepers' lips.

Many translations render v.1 as 'prince's daughter,' leading to speculation that this song was written in honour of the queen of Sheba. But 'prince' is actually the same word, 'nadib,' that is found in the phrase, 'the chariots of Ammi-nadib' (see 6:12 above). It's root meaning is 'willing,' or 'generous;' from which, in common usage, it came to mean one of noble character, or a nobleman. So it does not necessarily imply royal birth; and could even simply mean 'daughter of Nadib.'

Nevertheless, it is still quite possible that the Seeker's parents could have been regarded as a noble family even though she herself was held in low esteem, just as appears to have been the case with Jesse and David (see discussion on 1:6).

Do you notice something unusual about this particular description of the Seeker?

It begins with her feet and legs; then works upwards.

Now normally, when we meet someone, it is their face that draws our attention. So why her feet? OK, she has beautiful feet and nice sandals: but is that it? I think not.

Verse 7 suggests that she is standing, perhaps even with arms stretched out like the fronds of a palm tree. Now, given that they have just been comparing her to the dance of the two camps, I think the most likely reason is that she is *literally* dancing in sheer delight! So the king gazes in fascination at her twirling feet; then his eye travels admiringly upwards to her face, until he can restrain himself no longer and he rushes forward to embrace and kiss her again.

But the king's joy is not just in her new-found strength and exuberance. When he speaks of her 'delights,' in v. 6, the word implies that which is soft and delicate – even dainty. She retains a tenderness – a vulnerability and sensitivity towards him – that he finds deeply attractive.

Now it is the king's turn to compare her kisses with the best wine (v. 9). But the following words, '*It flows down smoothly for my beloved*,' use the word 'beloved' ('uncle' – see 1:16), which is her normal way of addressing him. So it seems that she is now responding to his words. The word translated 'smoothly' carries with it the sense of rightness and directness, as if she was saying, 'it goes down easily; because it is meant for you.'

Translating the last part of her reply is difficult, as the word '*dabab*,' variously rendered 'moving gently,' 'causing to speak' or 'strengthening,' occurs nowhere else. The balance of opinion seems to be that its primary meaning is 'moving gently.'

There is also debate about the word '*yashen*', translated as 'sleep'/'sleepers'. It comes from a root that can also, in some contexts, mean 'aged:' but this does not seem particularly appropriate here.

The ancient Septuagint version treats '*yashen*' (יָשֵׁן) as a copyist's error, substituting 'teeth' ('*shen*' – שֵׁן) to give, 'moving gently over lips and teeth.' Some modern versions do the same: but it's not a particularly striking image; and we don't know if the substitution was based on firm evidence or mere conjecture.

To say, 'moving gently *over* the lips of sleepers,' though grammatically correct, seems inappropriate – why would wine be flowing over the lips of someone who is asleep? On the other hand, 'moving gently the lips of sleepers,' invokes a powerful picture of one so completely overcome that, even in their sleep, they continue to murmur in delight.

So what does Jesus see when He looks at us?

He is thrilled when He sees us displaying uninhibited joy because of his presence and love for us. Worship and praise out of hearts overflowing with his love draws Him to us like nothing else. It was what He made us for; what He Himself suffered to accomplish. Indeed, our love is better than the best of wine to Him: and, though He never sleeps, in his delight He never stops murmuring your name –in fact, He sings it! (See Zeph 3:17.)

KEEPING CLOSE TO HIM (7:10-8:7)

Moving On in Love (7:10-13)

[10]I am my beloved's, and his desire is for me.
[11]Come, my beloved, let us go out into the field; let us lodge in the villages. [12]Let us get up early to the vineyards; let's see if the vine has sprouted, whether the grape blossom is opening, and the pomegranates bud forth: there I will give you my loves. [13]The mandrakes have given their fragrance; and at our doors are all choice things – new and old – which I have laid up for you, my beloved.

Here, at last, we see the Seeker not merely responding to the king's call to come with him to the fields and vineyards, but even suggesting it herself. How different she is now! But what exactly has changed?

She is now utterly confident that, whatever she may be called upon to do for him, it can never be as important to him as she herself is. *'His desire is for me.'* She wants to work alongside him, because she loves being with him: and now she is sure that he feels exactly the same way about her.

As a result, what was once drudgery, is now an opportunity. Once she was forced to work the vineyards, enduring the heat of the sun, because she was despised. Small wonder then that, to begin with, she had no desire to go back there, even in the company of the king. She had been hiding away from a painful past. But her past is now like a distant memory – blotted out by the knowledge of his passion for her. There will be more than mere labour – there will be opportunities for sharing, for intimacy, for love. The task itself does not seem to have changed much: but now it is no longer an obligation and a chore: it is a joyful choice.

It is an opportunity that she is determined to make the most of. Mandrakes were regarded as an aphrodisiac (their Hebrew name comes from the same stem as 'beloved.') And she has been busy making sure that she has plenty of good things ready for him – both literally and figuratively (the Hebrew text uses a word meaning 'excellent things' – not just fruit). Her love is stimulating her creativity, as she seeks new ways of pleasing her king: though with commendable wisdom she is careful to remember his known favourites.

It is so important for us to realise that the work we do for Jesus is always of secondary importance to Him: we ourselves matter to Him so much more. I do not serve Jesus in the hope of winning his approval. I serve Him because I am already so blessed by the unconditional love He has for me that I just want to take every opportunity I can to be near Him, sharing in his work and enjoying more of his love.

In our lives, we may still be doing much the same things as we used to do – same environment, same job, same commitments, etc. But once we are infected with this love of Jesus, that world is transformed. Every task provides an opportunity for us to perform it with Him, and for Him. Once that realisation truly gets hold of our hearts, instead of running from our circumstances, we will be eager to remain in them as long as He desires.

And, like her, we will not be content merely to perform the tasks He sets before us: but we will actively seek ways of bringing pleasure to his heart and enjoying times of personal intimacy with Him.

It is so important that we never let our service for Him slip into routine, and become task-oriented rather than love-oriented. So many Christians, especially church leaders, have fallen into that trap. Delight has fallen into drudgery once more, and Jesus' call to us to come and enjoy fellowship with Him has met with the response, 'I'm too tired just now. Later, when I feel like it, perhaps.' Before we know it, we're wondering where God has gone again...

Jesus also taught that *'every scribe who has been made a disciple in the Kingdom of Heaven is like a man who is a householder, who brings out of his treasure new and old things.'* (Mt 13:52.) God loves it when we are creative in finding new ways of expressing our love for Him; and it is good to change the way we do things from time to time in order to preserve the freshness and vitality of our worship and service. But balance is required.

Sadly, I have sometimes seen both individual Christians and even whole churches that, in over-reaction to a perceived stagnation in their lives, have abandoned their entire pattern of regular worship and waiting on God in favour of the latest success formula. Then, finding this was not all it was supposed to be, they have dropped that also and drifted around looking for something else.

Prove all things: hold fast that which is good (1 Thess 5:21). But do not strangle them by holding too tightly, or starve them by neglect.

An Intimacy that Cannot be Shared (8:1-3)

¹*Oh, that you were like my brother, who sucked my mother's breasts! If I met you in the street, I could kiss you; yet they would not despise me. ²I would lead you, and bring you into my mother's house, who would instruct me: I would cause you to drink spiced wine from the juice of my pomegranate.*

³*His left hand is under my head, and his right hand embraces me.*

> In many eastern cultures any public display of sexual attraction, even between husband and wife, is frowned upon: whereas shows of affection between friends and family may be regarded as perfectly acceptable.

In her yearning for intimacy, she finds that her actions are not always understood. Nor is it always appropriate for others to know all that passes between her and her king. This is both inevitable and frustrating: but there is only one practicable remedy; she must seek time alone with her king whenever she can and limit her public expression of her love. What passes between them in their private times together is so personal that only her mother, who knew and understood her so well, could ever be a confidante in such matters.

In the end, however, what passes between them is between him and her alone.

In natural love, the deeper and more intimate it becomes, the more sensitive each partner becomes to the personal nature of that sharing. The closer and more personal that sharing becomes the more it becomes a violation of trust to gossip about it to strangers, or even friends. It was for you and you alone. That was what made it so special: and any attempt to brag about it, or talk about it, can only cheapen it somehow.

True spirituality cannot be publicised any more than true human intimacy. Hence, Jesus taught, *'when you pray, enter into your inner room, and having shut your door, pray to your Father who is in secret, and your Father who sees in secret will reward you openly.'* (Mt 6:6.)

At times this can be deeply frustrating. There you are, just thrilled with the things Jesus has been showing you and doing in your life; and just longing to tell everyone all about it and shout his praises from the rooftops. Yet you know that those around you would simply not understand or, worse still, their attention would be focussed on you rather than your King. So all you can do for them at that moment is pray that one day they too will understand. And all you can do for yourself is pray silently; and long for your next chance to be alone with Him again.

> We must occasionally speak of such times in order to teach or encourage others. How would we have known about Jesus' 40 days in the wilderness if He had not told his disciples?
>
> But we must examine our motives carefully. Jesus taught that those who seek to proclaim their own spirituality have already received all the reward they are going to get. (Mt 6:5)

Love needs time alone together. Give Him plenty of it!

Don't Try to Rush It! (8:4)

⁴I have charged you, O daughters of Jerusalem: how you should not awaken or stir up love until it desires..

Yet again she cautions the daughters of Jerusalem about not wakening love until it pleases. But this time it differs from the other two occasions (2:7 and 3:5). There is the obvious omission of reference to the gazelles and does of the field. But the Hebrew text also reveals a subtle difference in the verb forms that is not easily translated and is glossed over in the majority of translations. Young's Literal Translation expresses the first two instances as 'stir not up, nor wake...,' and this last as, 'how ye stir up, and how ye wake....' The inference is that the narrative itself is a demonstration of what the admonition means.

We have noted that both previous admonitions were given during a time of deep intimacy. The first was when she had just found herself so utterly overwhelmed by love that she was at the end of her strength. The second was when she had been through an experience where, drawn by her yearning, she had to go out into the 'beyond' for her king. So in both cases, an experience that stretched her to her limits was followed by deep intimacy: but the second experience had stretched her far more than the first.

So where is she now? In a place of even deeper intimacy, after a period of even greater stretching. She has been deeply changed by all that she has gone through: changed to such an extent that she is now able to endure things that were unthinkable to her before; and with it she has found a level of trust and intimacy of which she previously had no concept.

Most of us desire a deeper relationship with God, as she did. But that does not mean that we are ready for it. Love is not easy or cheap: it will stretch us to our limits. It will change us: though in changing us it will make us richer and readier for more. A favourite author of mine, A.W. Tozer, once observed, 'It may be said without qualification that every man is as holy and as full of the Spirit as he wants to be. He may not be as full as he wishes he were, but he is most certainly as full as he wants to be.' (*Born After Midnight*, Christian Publications, Inc.)

But if we are not ready now that does not mean that we never will be. Rather, to recognise and admit our present need and unreadiness is the first step on the road to being made ready. And this narrative shows us how.

It begins with one who is deeply insecure; yet has a desire to be with the king. At that time she has no ambition to accompany him out into the wild places of the land – a banqueting hall sounds good to her, well away from those wretched vineyards! But he takes her desire, such as it is, and with patient, constant love encourages her and draws her out to ultimately become the kind of person he had seen her to be from the very first.

But this process takes time, and cannot be rushed. Love grows and increases at its own pace, as He works on our hearts. We like instant results: but we are dealing with the God who uses raindrops to carve mountains! He won't be hurried. We must learn to let Him deal with us in his way, at his pace.

So why did the other 2 verses refer to the gazelles and does? It is probably because they were seen as an illustration of this principle. The females will only mate at the appropriate season; and even so, they will not rush into a relationship. The male must first win their admiration by seeing off all the competition. Only then will they finally yield themselves to him. In the same way our Seeker held back until she had found the one lover that was worthy of all her love.

Transformed by Love (8:5-7)

⁵*Who is this coming up from the wilderness, leaning on her beloved? Beneath the apricot tree I roused you; there your mother was in labour; there she who was in labour gave you birth.*

⁶*Set me as a seal on your heart, as a seal on your arm. For love is as strong as death: passion as unyielding as Sheol; its burnings are like the burnings of fire, the flame of Yahweh! ⁷Many waters cannot quench love; rivers cannot sweep it away. (Even) if a man*

were giving all the riches of his house for love, it would (still) be
condemned as beneath contempt!

Finally, she is ready even to face the wilderness with her
king. And, as she returns from it with him, to visit her
birthplace, the transformation in her life is now so great that the
speaker, who appears to be a close family friend or relative
(perhaps even her own father), has difficulty recognising her.

But deeper commitment has taken her beyond the limits of
her own strength and brought deeper dependence. She leans on
her king for support now.

She knows that she
cannot live without his
love. She realises, too, that
love has the power to
transcend death itself:
true love is indestructible.
Compared to it, even all
the riches of a king are
contemptible. So, feeling
her own weakness, she
pleads with him for the
ongoing protection of his
love.

The deeper we go in
love with the Lord, the
more we will feel our
own weakness, and the
more we will depend
upon his strength.

Such things are easily
said: but the truth of it cuts
so deep. It doesn't matter

> Most translations contrast love with
> vengeful jealousy in this passage,
> and I initially did so too. But I now
> think the New International Version
> rendering is better.
>
> The word commonly translated as
> 'jealousy' also describes the passion
> of a husband for his wife, or of God
> for his people. And a study of the
> word often rendered as 'cruel'
> shows its primary meaning is
> unyielding hardness – a passion
> strong as death, so intense not even
> Sheol (the grave) can break or
> overpower it.
>
> The next words literally say this
> passion is like the flame of Jahweh
> himself. This similarly complements
> the statement, 'Many waters cannot
> quench love;' thus reinforcing,
> rather than negating, the total
> confidence she expresses in the
> protection of his love.

where you start from – as a downtrodden maiden with no
personal self-esteem or as a confident, 'can do anything' sort of
guy. Sooner or later you will learn that love can take you
anywhere. But that also means that it can take you to places that

are utterly beyond your own power to endure – places that you will only be able to go if you are totally dependent on his love.

So, even though your love is stronger than it has ever been before and, because of that you are stronger than you have ever been before, there will always be in your heart that desperate cry, 'Lord, hold me – I know I can't make it without you.' There will always be that sense of the incredible height to which He has lifted us, and the awful depth to which we could again plummet were it not for his keeping power.

But in, and through, and all around us there is this wonderful confidence: we know that we are secure. His love cannot fail, and his love has already conquered death and all of hell for us.

Compared to such love, nothing else in this world is of value. As Paul said, '*I count all things to be loss for the excellency of the knowledge of Christ Jesus, my Lord, for whom I suffered the loss of all things, and count them nothing but refuse, that I may gain Christ.*' (Phil 3:8.)

THE LEGACY OF LOVE (8:8-14)

Guiding and Guarding (8:8-10)

⁸We have a little sister, and she has no breasts. What shall we do for our sister in the day when she is spoken for? ⁹If she is a wall, we will build on her a battlement of silver: and if she is a door, we will shut her in with boards of cedar.

¹⁰I am a wall, and my breasts like towers: then, in his eyes, I was like one finding peace.

Some onlookers (perhaps her relatives, or the Daughters of Jerusalem) then raise a question that relates back to the Seeker's earlier exhortation, 'Do not stir up nor awaken love until it pleases.' They have a little sister who plainly is not yet ready for love or marriage. But how should they treat her when she reaches an age at which she could be?

Note that, in their society, the family would normally be expected to assume responsibility for ensuring that she was married to a suitable husband. Many marriages would have been arranged by the parents. (This does not appear to have been the case for the Seeker, who was chosen by the King: but then, no parent would have been likely to object to such a match!)

The answer they give is couched metaphorically: is she a 'wall' type or a 'door' type? What does this signify? There are two important clues.

Firstly, the Seeker describes herself as a 'wall' type: so a 'wall' type is good. If their sister is like this, they say they will construct a battlement or walled dwelling of silver on her. The Seeker likens her breasts to towers upon the wall, and emphasises the favour she has received.

Secondly, there is strong evidence that a 'door' type is not good. Not only does wood, even cedar wood, not come anywhere near silver in value: but the word translated as 'shut in' does not simply mean 'cover;' it means 'to confine,' 'lay siege to,' 'distress,' or even 'show hostility towards.' So it looks as if their response is not going to be something she would like.

So what's the crucial difference? Walls keep people out: doors let people in.

The king described the Seeker as being like an enclosed garden, private, reserved. She had been resolved not to give herself to anyone until she found the one who merited her love. He, and he alone, would be permitted to dwell between her breasts and occupy her heart.

The relatives are saying that, if their sister proves to be of such a disposition, they will do all they can to help her become a worthy bride. But, conversely, if she proved to have a disposition that would easily yield to anyone who sought to entice her, then they would take all necessary measures to prevent it, even if this were painful for her.

If we think back to the exhortation not to stir up or awaken love 'until it pleases,' it is possible to see that there are two main ways in which this could be ignored to someone's cost.

One danger is that of seeking to enter into a love relationship before you are truly ready for it. Many failed romances might have prospered had more time been given for those involved to mature in their attitudes to one another.

But the other, and probably more common, danger is that of being too eager in the quest for love; and accepting that which is less than it should be. Ultimately, if their little sister were to do this, she would be the loser; so, whatever the present pain, her family are resolved that she should not suffer this misfortune. Love is far too precious to pledge or sacrifice on impulse.

We have a deep responsibility for the spiritual well-being of the next generation: and they are facing massive pressure to give themselves to all kinds of false loves. We need to do all we can to encourage and disciple those who have a genuine desire to put God first.

We should also do all in our power to deter those who would commit themselves too soon; so that, by God's grace, they may discover in time the true and lasting love that can only be found through Him.

We may not be popular for doing so: but the risks are too high for us to simply stand back and say, 'They can learn from their own mistakes.'

> We should seek to deter foolish behaviour. But as our children grow older there is a limit to how much we can, or should, compel.
>
> The Prodigal Son's father did not have to give the inheritance money to his son. He took a big risk in doing so: but the son's eventual decision to return demonstrates that the mercy and fairness demonstrated by his father had not been in vain.

Possessing the Beyond (8:11)

[11] *Solomon had a vineyard at Baal-hamon. He let the vineyard out to keepers; for its fruit each man would bring a thousand in silver.*

Solomon had a magnificent vineyard, which he rented out. It must have been very fruitful, as those who leased it were prepared to pay handsomely for the privilege. But what is particularly interesting is its location. Some identify it with Belamon, near Dothan, in the hills north of Samaria; which is a considerable distance from Jerusalem. But probably the most likely location is Baal-Hermon. This was even farther away, at the very northernmost limits of his kingdom.

The significance of this is that it demonstrates that the king was no mere visitor in such distant regions: he was determined to posess them and make them fruitful.

Jesus is the same. He doesn't just take us through the wilderness: He makes it fruitful! As the scriptures say, '*The wilderness and the dry land will be glad. The desert will rejoice and blossom like a rose.*' (Is. 35:1.) '*Passing through the valley of Weeping, they make it a place of springs. Yes, the autumn rain covers it with blessings.'* (Ps. 84:6.)

And He also takes possession. In Psalm 2:8 the Father prophetically declares concerning Jesus, *'Ask of me, and I will give the nations for your inheritance, the uttermost parts of the earth for your possession.'* (Ps. 2:8.) Then in Matthew 28:18-19 Jesus says, *'All authority has been given to me in heaven and on earth. Go, and make disciples of all nations...'*

Our destiny is not to be ruled by situations: but to take posession of them with Him and then see them change and become fruitful.

Remembering and Sharing (8:12)

¹²My vineyard – my (very) own – is before me. For you, Solomon, – a thousand! And for the keepers of its fruit – two hundred.

Do you remember the Seeker's earlier complaint? *'They made me keeper of the vineyards: but my own vineyard I have not kept.'* (1:6.) She remembers well enough what it was like to toil in the sun, caring for a vineyard that wasn't hers; almost certainly, in her case, not even getting paid for it.

Now, her circumstances are dramatically changed: she has been given her very own vineyard, to do as she pleases with! Is this the vineyard of Solomon we have just heard about? If so, then she too now has posessions in the land where she once feared even to tread.

But look at the way she responds to this blessing.

Firstly, even though the vineyard has been given as her very own possession; she **chooses** to pay the same tribute to Solomon as his own tenants do. By this she acknowledges that all she is, and all she has, she owes to Him; and she will not let anyone out-give her. They may be doing it out of necessity: but she is not. Rather, she will not be out-given **because she is doing it out of love**.

And she doesn't stop there. She remembers too the hard times of her youth and is determined that her workers will not be treated as she was: they, too, will be paid handsomely!

How much more do we owe to our Lord?! How can we hold on to the good things He has given us, keeping them for ourselves, when all of them came from Him? In truth, I think most of us, myself included, still hold on to rather more than we should; and there are some professing Christians who seem little different from unbelievers in this respect. But that only serves to underline the difference between one who claims to know the love of Christ, and one who has truly experienced it. The more you experience, the more you long to bless Him in return.

Why do some people argue about whether Christians should tithe 10% of their income or not? Do we have to do this? No!!! It was obligatory only under the law of Moses: yet Abraham and Jacob did it voluntarily (Gen 14:20, 28:22). And who wants to hold back from giving whatever they can to Jesus just to prove that they are 'not under law'?

On the other hand, if your heart is to give even more if you could, but just now you feel imprisoned by your circumstances and unable to give even that much, take heart. The God who promised blessing on his poverty-stricken people, if they would but bring their tithes as an act of obedience and faith (Mal 3:10), has not changed. If He blesses those who give out of obligation, how much more will He bless those who give out of love?

Any real experience of the love of God does not merely make us love God more: it makes us love people more as well. The more we experience of God's transformation in us, the more it encourages a sense of empathy with those who still are as we once were. As his nature mingles with ours, we find that we cannot help but share in his desire to love and to bless.

So John writes that it is impossible for us to love God if we don't love our fellow-man, whom God made in his own image. And James writes scathingly of the futility of professions of faith that do not express their love in practical compassion.

I fear that many of us have too often missed the plot here. We know that loving the King is what matters most: but we are apt to overlook the fact that there is a proper and vitally important place for simply promoting kindness and justice, man-to-man.

When I became a Christian, in the 1960's, there was an influential trend in the church, often referred to as the 'social gospel.' As its name implied, it emphasised the importance of these social issues. Tragically, however, it frequently did so as a substitute for proclaiming the life-changing power of Jesus' death and resurrection: with the result that for many Christians the term 'social gospel' came to be seen as almost synonymous with apostasy – a diversionary tactic of Satan to be carefully avoided.

But the reality is that this was always a central part of Jesus' own teaching and practice. The Sermon on the mount is packed with teaching on social justice. And caring for the poor was such an integral part of Jesus' own ministry that, when Jesus sent Judas out during the last supper, the other apostles thought nothing of it. Judas was the group's treasurer; so perhaps he was just taking a gift to someone in need (Jn 13:27-29).

Sometimes we compromise by mostly just giving to the 'deserving.' But Jesus did not do this. He healed ten lepers: only one returned to give thanks (Luke 17:12-18). He fed 5,000 men, plus women and children: but by the time He had finished explaining the importance of a personal commitment to Himself, all but a handful turned their backs on Him (John 6:1-67). Knowing the hearts of men as He did, He would have realised how these people were likely to respond (see John 2:25). Yet He saw their need, and gave anyway.

We need to remember where we ourselves have come from, and what it felt like to be there. As disciples of Jesus, we should be concerned for all men, whether we think them deserving or not: for it was when we were at our most undeserving that Jesus died for us (Rom 5:6-8).

Urging Each Other On (8:13-14)

[13]*You who dwell in the gardens, (your) companions are attentive to your voice: cause me to hear it.*

[14]*Make haste, my beloved; and be like a gazelle or a young hart on the mountains of spices!*

The king does not cease being the shepherd king just because he is married! But neither does she accompany him on every trip, just because she is his bride and has been to the wilderness with him once. The song closes with him taking his leave of his bride as he prepares for another journey.

He encourages her that he will be listening out for the sound of her voice as he leaves or returns – probably both! She, for her part urges him to hasten away (in other contexts, this word is frequently translated as 'flee'). The quicker he goes, the sooner he will be back! Nevertheless, she accepts and delights in his outgoing character. Far from trying to restrain him, she urges him on with words of admiration.

Both are clearly anticipating their next reunion...

By finally reaching the point where she was able and willing to accompany the king into the far regions, the Seeker has reached a deep understanding and empathy with the things that he is doing. But, clearly, that does not mean that she has suddenly become the 'outdoor type,' complete with rucksack and climbing boots! She still prefers to stay at home, doing more feminine things.

True love does not mean that we cease to be individuals or become carbon copies of each other. Some religions see perfection as a loss of personal identity: but the biblical teaching, as here, is that we retain our special attributes; learning to appreciate our differences and encouraging each other to fulfil all our potential in God.

Part of that process is that we should never take each other's love for granted. Take a poor man into a posh restaurant, and he will wonder if he is in heaven: take a rich man, and he will think nothing of it. We have this tendency to become familiar even with the most wonderful things, so that we cease to really appreciate or even notice them.

If we are not careful of this, we can all too easily neglect even the very best things and allow them to slip away from us. So it is important that we cultivate a pattern of appreciativeness and mutual encouragement in our lives. I do not know how many thousand times I have told my wife, 'I love you,' over the last thirty years: but I do know that, if I ever were to stop, our relationship would be so much poorer for it.

This is equally true in our relationship with God. He, for his part is constantly saying 'I love you,' through his Word, and through the countless blessings He sends on us day by day. As we noted at the beginning, it's the way He loves us – not just the fact that He does – that stirs up our own love.

But if we do not take time to regularly read his Word or appreciate his gifts we will be like a young woman who daily received love letters and chocolates from her young admirer: yet simply ate the chocolates without opening the letters or even reading the labels.

Nor should we ever lose sight of just how precious our love is to Jesus.

You are his treasure. It was for the joy of knowing your love that He endured the cross; and nothing in all of creation thrills Him more than to hear you say, 'I love You. I love spending time with You.' Let that realization grip your soul more and more and you will find yourself saying such things with ever-increasing frequency and intensity.

True love is never prepared to stop and say, 'That's enough.' There is always a desire for more, always room for more and always a need for us to keep on encouraging and provoking that desire in one another.

Our Jesus will never cease to be the Shepherd King, and will never cease to thrill us with the things He has done and will yet do. Yet He will never cease to be thrilled with our love, small as it may be in comparison with his, and will never cease to take delight in the voice of our praise and hasten to be with us again, throughout the ages of eternity.

EPILOGUE

When I first began sharing from this book about the passion of the King for his bride, I found myself asking, 'Lord, am I overstating this? Am I being too fanciful when I try to describe the effect that our love has on you?' In response, He showed me the following beautiful demonstration of its truth...

Heaven Can Wait!

Jn 20:11But Mary was standing outside at the tomb weeping. So, as she wept, she stooped and looked into the tomb, 12and she saw two angels in white sitting, one at the head, and one at the feet, where the body of Jesus had lain. 13They told her, "Woman, why are you weeping?"

She said to them, "Because they have taken away my Lord, and I don't know where they have laid him." 14When she had said this, she turned around and saw Jesus standing, and didn't know that it was Jesus.

15Jesus said to her, "Woman, why are you weeping? Who are you looking for?"

She, supposing him to be the gardener, said to him, "Sir, if you have carried him away, tell me where you have laid him, and I will take him away."

16Jesus said to her, "Mary."

She turned and said to him, "Rabboni !" which is to say, "Teacher !"

*17Jesus said to her, "**Don't hold me, for I haven't yet ascended to my Father**; but go to my brothers, and tell them, 'I am ascending to my Father and your Father, to my God and your God.'"*

...

^{Mt 28:9} *As they went to tell his disciples, behold, Jesus met them, saying, "Rejoice!"*

*They came and **took hold of his feet**, and worshiped him.*

When Jesus meets Mary, He does not let her touch Him: but when He meets the other women, He lets them hold his feet. Why this difference? The answer is there in the detail of the gospel accounts: and it is awe-inspiring!

Why does John only mention Mary Magdalene in his account of that morning? She was not alone when she went to the tomb; for when she found Peter and John she told them, *"**We** don't know where they have laid him!"* (Jn 20:2 *cf.* Mt 28:1, Mk 16:1 & Lk 24:10).

It seems that, on finding the empty tomb, the women split up. Peter and John were separated from the others on the night of Jesus' arrest and remained so on the crucifixion day[1]. John had contacts in Jerusalem, so it is likely that he and Peter lodged in the city while the other disciples stayed at the house of Mary and Martha in Bethany.

Thus Mary could find and bring Peter and John back to the tomb within minutes, while the other women were still on their way to Bethany to tell the other disciples.

But where is Jesus?

He is still watching and waiting, close by the tomb.

Now let me change perspective, and look at this unfolding drama from heaven's viewpoint.

Heaven has just come to the end of what must have been the darkest moment in all eternity. The glorious, immaculate Son of God, whom all the angels worshipped, the prime object of the Father's love, had been beaten and cruelly murdered at the hands of men. Mighty warrior angels had stood, horrified, yearning for one word of command that would free them to

---

[1]   Only Peter and John followed Jesus to the house of Caiaphas (Jn 18:15-16). Most of the disciples watched the crucifixion from a safe distance (Lk 23:49): but John was standing by the cross (Jn 19:25-27). We don't know where Peter was at this point.

swoop down to rescue Him and take vengeance! But, worse than that, the Father Himself had been forced to turn away from Jesus as, weighted down with our sins, He slipped away out of sight into the abyss of Sheol.

How can we begin to imagine the grief and mourning there must have been in heaven during those dreadful three days of our time?

But what a party they were preparing now!

All over heaven the shout would have gone up, "He has risen!" Every inhabitant of heaven would be watching, waiting, for the moment when the Risen, Exalted, Beloved Son of God, would enter through heaven's gates to present Himself victorious before the Father. Angels, with trumpets to their lips, would be bracing themselves to sound the loudest fanfare of triumph heaven had ever heard ...

... And they waited...

... And waited...

Where is Jesus?

He is still watching and waiting, close by the tomb.

But why?

Because Mary is weeping.

Peter and John are wondering, and beginning to believe. The other women are frightened: but excited by what they have seen. Jesus will appear to them in a little while, after He has been to the Father.

But Mary is weeping. The One she loved most in all the world has been taken from her. She does not understand. Even if all she can have is his dead body, then that is all she wants. Nothing else matters to her.

And because nothing else matters to her, no-one else matters more to Jesus.

Heaven can wait!

So Jesus turns aside for Mary. He will not let her touch Him; for He is determined that no-one but the Father shall be first to embrace Him on that resurrection morning. But the celebrations in heaven must be put on hold until she is comforted.

Even the Father must wait. He will understand. For He knows that Jesus endured the agony of the cross for this very thing – to have a people that would seek to love Him as passionately as He Himself loved them.

Am I overstating how much Mary's passion meant to Him? No. For although Jesus will not let Mary touch Him, because He has not yet ascended, He raises no such objection with the other women. The implication is clear: it was *only for Mary* that heaven waited that day.

But what was it that made Mary's love so special? Not physical attraction, as some have tried to suggest, or surely He would have waited until He could hold her. Yet, when we compare Mary with the Seeker of Solomon's Song, the parallels are obvious.

> It is difficult for us to reconcile the timelessness of heaven with the time-scales of earth. The time lapse between the resurrection and Jesus' meeting with Mary was probably only about 15 minutes.
>
> Yet, in the few minutes of our time between this and his meeting with the other women, who knows how many minutes, hours or even aeons He spent in the Father's loving embrace?

This is not Mary the immaculate: it is Mary the ex-demoniac (Lk 8:2), the despised one. But she who is forgiven much loves much (Lk 7:47)[1]. Like the Seeker, she no longer cared who knew about her love or what they thought of her. She was past putting up any kind of front to cover up her desperation for Him: He was all she wanted.

To Jesus, such love is irresistible. And the only qualification you need to reach that place from wherever you are now is that you begin by appreciating his love for you.

His love will take care of all the rest…

---

[1] Mary is often said to be the woman in Lk 7:37-50: though Luke does not say so when he first mentions her in Lk 8:2. It was Mary, Lazarus' sister, who performed a similar act just before Jesus' death in Jn 12:1-8 (*cf.* Jn 11:2).

Has this book been a blessing to you?

If so, why not share that blessing with someone else?

It has been my desire that as many people as possible should benefit from the lessons I have learnt in this book. For this reason I have funded publication myself so that it could be reproduced as freely and cheaply as practicable in both electronic and printed form.
But I also have to live and raise money for ongoing ministry; and to make printed copies available for those who cannot afford them or access on-line sources. So here are some ways you can help:

- Buy copies for your friends. This will not only bless them: but the revenue generated will be a means of further blessing to myself and others.
- Lend it. Electronic copies may be circulated freely, subject to any restrictions imposed by the distribution channel through which your copy was obtained.
- Recommend it. Using the 'Like' buttons on Facebook, Twitter, Amazon, etc. is a great way of sharing the message. And if you've got time to write a brief review, that's even better!

For more information, please visit:
http://transformed-by-love.com

www.ingramcontent.com/pod-product-compliance
Lightning Source LLC
Chambersburg PA
CBHW031901090426
42741CB00005B/586